riend By Day, Enemy By Night

GANIZED VENGEANCE IN A KOHISTANI COMMUNITY

oln Keiser

CENGAGE
Learning™

Australia • Brazil • Japan • Korea • Mexico • Singapore • Spain • United Kingdom • United States

CENGAGE
Learning™

Friend By Day, Enemy By Night: Organized Violence in a Kohistani Community

Lincoln Keiser

Executive Editors:
Michele Baird

Maureen Staudt

Michael Stranz

Project Development Manager:
Linda deStefano

Senior Marketing Coordinators:
Sara Mecurio

Lindsay Shapiro

Production/Manufacturing Manager:
Donna M. Brown

PreMedia Services Supervisor:
Rebecca A. Walker

Rights & Permissions Specialist:
Kalina Hintz

Cover Image:
Getty Images*

For product information and technology assistance, contact us at **Cengage Learning Customer & Sales Support, 1-800-354-9706**

For permission to use material from this text or product, submit all requests online at **cengage.com/permissions** Further permissions questions can be emailed to **permissionrequest@cengage.com**

ISBN-13: 978-0-03-053332-7

ISBN-10: 0-03-053332-5

Cengage Learning

5191 Natorp Boulevard
Mason, Ohio 45040
USA

Cengage Learning is a leading provider of customized learning solutions with office locations around the globe, including Singapore, the United Kingdom, Australia, Mexico, Brazil, and Japa Locate your local office at: **international.cengage.com/region**

Cengage Learning products are represented in Canada by Nelson Education, Ltd.

For your lifelong learning solutions, visit **custom.cengage.com**

Visit our corporate website at **cengage.com**

Printed in the United States of America

Dedicated to the memory of Dr. Mohammad Rauf

Foreword

ABOUT THE SERIES

These case studies in cultural anthropology are designed to bring to students, in beginning and intermediate courses in the social sciences, insights into the richness and complexity of human life as it is lived in different ways and in different places. They are written by men and women who have lived in the societies they write about and who are professionally trained as observers and interpreters of human behavior. The authors are also teachers, and in writing their books they have kept the students who will read them foremost in their minds. It is our belief that when an understanding of ways of life very different from one's own is gained, abstractions and generalizations about social structure, cultural values, subsistence techniques, and the other universal categories of human social behavior become meaningful.

ABOUT THE AUTHOR

Lincoln Keiser was born in 1937 in Janesville, Wisconsin. He is one of eight children, three of whom are step siblings. As a child he explored the American Museum of Natural History during a family trip to New York City, an experience that initiated his interest in anthropology. He attended Lawrence College (now Lawrence University), graduating with a B.A. in anthropology in 1959. He received his M.A. degree in cultural anthropology from Northwestern University in 1964, and his Ph.D. in social anthropology from the University of Rochester in 1971.

Keiser's research focuses on the Hindu-Kush region of Afghanistan and Pakistan, and he has published articles on Hindu-Kush ethnography in various books and journals. He has also done research in the United States, publishing *Hustler: The Autobiography of a Thief* in 1965, and *The Vice Lords,* which appeared in this series in 1969. Presently he teaches anthropology at Wesleyan University. He is the father of one daughter.

ABOUT THIS CASE STUDY

Friend by Day, Enemy by Night explores blood feuding (*mar dushmani,* literally 'death enmity') and its ramifications in Thull, a Kohistani tribal community in the Hindu-Kush Mountains of Pakistan. The study shows how *mar dusmani* has come to interpenetrate life in this isolated community of mountaineers. Beliefs in the nature of God, concepts of self, patterns of ecological adaptation, the structure of houses, the number and kinds of dogs men own, the kinship and political system—death enmity penetrates and twists all these and more.

Men kill each other for numerous reasons in Thull; many appear trivial to the outsider. Staring at someone's wife or daughter, looking at her through a camera, or even reflecting light on her from a snuff box mirror cast aspersions on a man's honor, his *ghrairat,* and demand assassination. "Friend by day, enemy by night" is no idle phrase. Men may joke with each other during the day, and communicate with bullets at night. Houses are built with few or no windows, and chimneys rather than smoke holes so enemies, bent on revenge, cannot shoot into them. Men go about armed with all manner of weapons, including assault rifles such as the renowned AK 47. And, they are ready and willing to use them.

Limiting internal violence is essential for the continued existence of human communities. In acephalous societies like Thull, those lacking police, the judiciary, or centralized authority, controlling violence tends to be ambiguous under all conditions. Even in acephalous societies, though, when people exceed tolerable levels of violence their community usually disintegrates. Thull appears to be a society on the brink of disintegrating. And yet, in spite of a level of violence that seems intolerable to the outsider, life in Thull goes on.

The author, Lincoln Keiser, describes this life and the place of the individual in it. He explores how blood feuding came to infect social relations in Thull from a historical perspective, as well as studying its consequences for Thull society and culture. His analysis of the interrelationship of self and other in the framework of Kohistani meanings, especially the concepts of honor, revenge, feuding, and sociality are especially interesting.

Keiser concludes *Friend by Day, Enemy by Night* by sharing with us his personal experiences and reactions in fieldwork. Treated as a scheming outsider, an infidel capable of any dispicable behavior, despised by most Kohistanis, he nevertheless managed to do serious and credible research. His account of fieldwork is frank, giving us a different picture of the field experience than most of us have provided our readers, but one probably shared by most ethnographers in some ways.

This case study will take its place with the author's *The Vice Lords* as one of the most interesting and useful studies in the series.

GEORGE AND LOUISE SPINDLER
Series Editors
Ethnographics, Calistoga, California

Acknowledgments

Thanks are owed to Shamsher Ali Khan, Commissioner of the Malakand Agency, and other officials of the Pakistani Government who took time from busy schedules to assist scholarly research; to my research assistant, Shahid Mahmood, and his wife Abida; and to Makhbul, Said Akbar, Izzat Gul, Bakhtawan, Gul Sher, Hazrat Omar, Akbar Khan, and Dilawar Khan, informants whose help was obviously indispensable. I have changed their names and the names of all others appearing in the book to protect their privacy. I also wish to thank Bruce Lohaf, Director of U.S.E.F. in Pakistan for his invaluable aid and support. Julé Crawford, Jennifer Como, Lael Keiser, and the students in my 1989 political anthropology class all made valuable suggestions for improving the manuscript. The faith, encouragement, and criticism of George and Louise Spindler, editors of the Case Studies Series, were invaluable. Finally, I would like to thank Mohammad Rauf, my friend and colleague at Quaid-i-Azam University, whose support made my research possible. This book is dedicated to his memory. Research in Pakistan was supported by the Smithsonian Institution Grant 40250400.

Portions of the book have appeared earlier: in "Death Enmity in Thull," *American Ethnologist* 13 (1986); "Rimshots and Rifle Fire," *Natural History* 95 (1986); and "Friend by Day, Enemy by Night," *Natural History* 96 (1987).

Contents

FIGURES

MAPS

1 / Introduction

Field Diary: May 28, 1984

At eleven o'clock this morning Qai Afsal left after exchanging gossip and requesting medicine for his wife's illness. When he reached the road rifle shots rang from the high mesa dominating the approach to my house. Even though the bullets hit close to his feet, Qai Afsal sauntered down the road with his usual swagger.

Field Diary: June 4, 1984

At seven fifteen this evening the sound of automatic fire from AK-47 assault rifles interrupted my supper. The shots came from Kallan where Qai Afsal lives. The fire fight lasted about thirty minutes. About eight o'clock a jeep arrived in front of my house with Qai Afsal lying on the back seat, writhing in agony. Two bullets had hit him, but fortunately both had exited without damaging a vital organ or bone. After I had bandaged his wounds my driver drove him to the hospital in Peshawar.

Field Diary: June 15, 1984

Qai Afsal returned from the hospital today, vowing *badal* ("revenge"). Though community leaders plan *jirgas* ("public councils") to encourage a peaceful end to the fighting, no one believes Qai Afsal will forego revenge.

Field Diary: June 20, 1984

On June 17th, while I was in Islamabad, another pitched battle erupted between Qai Afsal, supported by his *ju* (literally "brothers," but in this case paternal cousins) and their enemies. Qai Afsal and his kinsmen successfully defended themselves because they possessed more automatic rifles than their attackers. The fight lasted about three hours. Tracers lit the sky and bullets flew in all directions from early evening until well after dark.

I wrote these field journal entries while conducting research in Thull, a Kohistani tribal community in the Hindu-Kush Mountains of Pakistan. They illustrate the importance of *mar dushmani* ("death enmity"—the Kohistani phrase for social relationships of blood vengeance) in the life of the community.

One cannot live in Thull even for a day without becoming aware of the pervasiveness of organized violence. The array of weaponry itself astounds the imagination—a genuine storehouse of arms. Men own specially made fighting knives, axes, clubs, walking sticks designed to double as stabbing spears, automatic pistols, revolvers, bolt-action rifles, updated versions of 19th-century British cavalry carbines, and the prize pieces: Kalashnikov AK-47 assault rifles. One even finds bolt-action versions of the AK-47, designed and produced by the local cottage arms industry. The sounds of Thull reflect its weaponry: rifle shots fill the air day and night. Religious authorities almost succeeded in stamping out singing and drumming; in their place gunfire became the music of Thull.

Reading Evans-Pritchard's *The Nuer* as a graduate student in 1965, I was intrigued by the way acephalous societies (those with no centralized political authority and few, if any, specialized political institutions) organize violence. This question focused my research both with the Vice Lords, a Black gang in Chicago, and with the Sum, a Kohistani community in the Hindu-Kush mountains on the Afghan side of the border. Subsequent reading of the ethnographic literature on Kohistani communities in Pakistan posed intriguing questions about blood feud violence. Among the tribes of Indus Kohistan, for example, organized revenge, in association with highly complex notions of personal honor, systematizes intracommunity political relationships. In contrast, among many of the Indo-Aryan tribes inhabiting the higher valleys to the west of the Indus, the value of maintaining communal harmony is generally unquestioned and so is a potent political force within the communities. I planned my research in Pakistan to focus on these differences, intending to begin by studying a community that forbade blood feuding.

Finding *dushmani* so entrenched in Thull surprised me. An early report had led me to believe its people generally settled their internal disputes without bloodshed. Further research revealed that the obsession with *dushmani* warping contemporary social relations there had developed only in the last few decades. Before then, most fights had opposed descent groups but had not involved deadly weapons. Now most fights oppose either individual antagonists alone or adversaries supported by various kinds of allies. Enemies attempt to kill one another to avenge personal injury, and no rules limit the use of weapons. I could find no written statistics on the number of murders committed in the community, although the leader of the small contingent of police in Thull did tell me revenge killings averaged two per month during his tenure. With a shake of his head he declared the people of Kohistan to be among the most lawless in Pakistan. The men of Thull, he added, are the most lawless in all of Kohistan. The change in customary behavior posed interesting questions about blood feud violence in acephalous societies, and consequently I chose to work in Thull.

I saw few women's faces and talked to none in the time I lived in Kohistan. Even my landlords' wives always appeared before me wearing the customary black, translucent cloth covering their faces. I could not pursue the female side of Kohistani culture, therefore, and my understanding of organized vengeance is incomplete. I am certain that women are more than passive objects in blood feud disputes, but I could learn nothing about their participation.

Originally I had hoped to breach the wall separating men from women in Thull by hiring a Pakistani husband/wife team as research assistants. This failed. Although the woman in the team formed intimate relations with the women in our household, she rarely left our house to visit other women because of *purdah* (the seclusion of women). This limited her work with me primarily to domestic chores even though she was very intelligent—a university graduate with a Master of Arts degree in anthropology. As a result my research was limited to the male perspective.

Male and female worlds in Thull are clearly demarcated and hierarchically ranked. The lines between them can be crossed only with great difficulty, if at all. Kohistani women do not own animals, and cannot herd them; they do not own guns, and cannot fight. They cannot enter mosques, and cannot hold positions of political authority. Accordingly I have used sex-specific terms throughout the text when discussing gender-limited activities to avoid distorting Kohistani society and culture.

THULL IN SPACE AND TIME

One finds Thull, a community of approximately six thousand Muslims, in the uppermost reaches of the Panjkora Valley, where the only road becomes a mountain track. A traveler cannot find a more remote community in Dir Kohistan. Dir District, of which Dir Kohistan forms a part, comprises

Thull Proper

The satellite district of Jo Thull

a section of Pakistan's Northwest Frontier Province. Chitral borders it in the north, Swat in the west, Afghanistan and Bajour in the east, and Malakand in the south.

Thull lies along some 40 kilometers of river valley. It includes a core village, fifteen satellite districts, and twenty-eight summer pasture areas. I first lived in Thull Proper, the core village, and then Lhul, one of the fifteen satellite districts, where houses lie scattered among fields and trees.

The people of Thull make their living by a mix of farming and herding. Traditionally women bore primary responsibility for farming, while men herded goats, cattle, water buffalo, and sheep. When potatoes were introduced as a cash crop, the division of labor changed so that men now dominate the agricultural dimension of subsistence as well.

Thull is remarkable for its distinctive sights and sounds. The following is what I wrote in my field journal on May 28, 1984, as I looked from my house in Lhul.

> Terraced fields in a succession of steps fall toward the Panjkora River. As one approaches the river the fields become relatively large, perhaps 30 yards long by 15 yards wide. Areas of grass, where an occasional cow placidly grazes, separate the fields. Chickens, goats, cows, donkeys, sheep, all seem to wander freely, neither tied nor fenced. Near the river stone terraces do not exist; low mud banks mark the boundaries of fields there.
>
> Some people, two men and a woman, break the ground with a hoelike implement in a field close to the river. Children play at the field's edge. Across the river

SOUTHWEST ASIA AND THE NORTHERN AREAS OF PAKISTAN

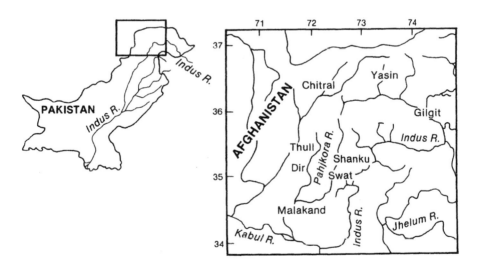

one can see the buildings of Kinorlam village dug into the mountainside. Some, probably barns, have grass roofs. Small groves of carefully planted trees dot the landscape. Clusters of graves surrounded by split-rail and thorn-bush fences scatter among the fields. Two-story houses lie next to the scatter of graves. Builders have plastered their walls with mud wattle, although they have left some with alternate layers of stone and wood exposed.

The gigantic Hindu-Kush mountains surrounding the valley make people seem insignificant. Dense forests still cling to many of her peaks, although timbering

Sketch map of Thull not drawn to scale

――― Boundary Line

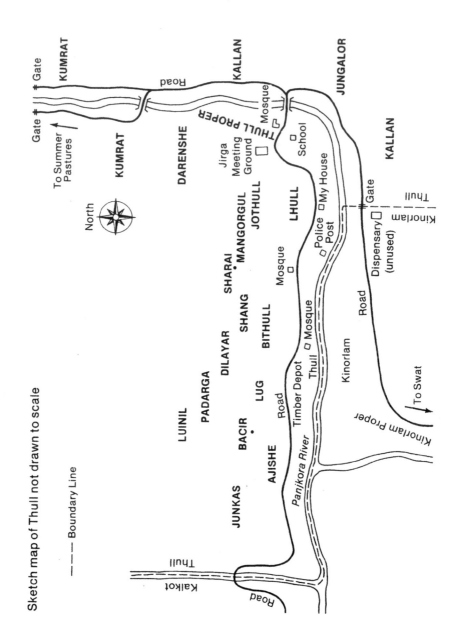

has taken its toll. In back of the main village rises a high ridge with thirteen peaks above the timber line, all clothed in eternal snow.

Just above my house, away from the river, the road unwinds. Groups of people and an occasional timber truck make their way along the road. Sometimes, a solitary woman with her face and body covered with a long black shawl glides effortlessly along the road with a load of wood, or a basket of stones on her head. Children—filthy, ragged for the most part, and many with running noses—dart over, around, and under everything in sight. Rifle shots and the braying of donkeys upset the peace. The night is rent by the continual barking of dogs. Their sound communicates a strong desire to rend limb from limb. Underneath it all, the hiss and roar of the swiftly flowing Panjkora forms a never-ending backdrop.

Indo-Aryan-speaking pagan tribes inhabited the northern, most remote valleys of Dir and Swat before the 15th century. Local traditions hint at the general political unrest endemic in Kohistan at the time. Inhabitants scattered their settlements high in the mountains to protect against raiders seeking plunder and avaricious neighbors seeking land and animals. One can still find the occasional remains of their villages today in inaccessible hollows, ravines, ridges, and small plateaus. Each community bore the responsibility for its own defense, and each allied with its neighbors for mutual protection. The inhabitants living on either side of the valley above the present location of Thull signaled impending danger with smoke signals, and joined to fight off invaders.

Events in Afghanistan during the last half of the 14th century set in motion ripple effects that profoundly altered Kohistani culture and society. A politically powerful Muslim tribe called the Khakhai inhabited the Kabul Valley during the reign of Ulugh Beg, the grandson of the great Turkish conqueror Tamerlane. Tensions between the unruly Khakhai and Ulugh Beg grew to the point of open conflict. To rid himself of this threat to his power, Ulugh Beg invited the most influential Khakhai leaders to a feast where his soldiers treacherously slaughtered them all. The tribe fled the Kabul valley after the massacre, and in the following decades steadily migrated to the east. The Yusufzai, a subdivision of the Khakhai, conquered lower Dir and Swat in the beginning of the 14th century. By 1550 they extended their control over the most fertile sections of both valleys.

Though unsuccessful in subjugating the Indo-Aryan pagan tribes in their inaccessible mountain retreats, the Yusufzai conquest nevertheless caused significant changes in Kohistani society and culture. New communities in Kohistan formed as Muslim refugees fleeing the Yusufzai invaders mingled with, and sometimes displaced, the pagan population. Muslim missionaries accompanied the refugees, converting most people to Islam even in the remote mountain valleys. They established themselves as religious authorities in the mountain communities around the year 1580.

During the next three centuries continually shifting political alliances and oppositions typified political relations in the region. Predatory attacks and counterattacks marked relationships between the communities in Kohistan and the emerging states in neighboring valleys. Kohistani raiders plundered villages in Yasin, Chitral, and Dir, while the villages in Kohistan were subjected to raids and small-scale invasions in return. In spite of continual attempts to conquer them, the Kohistanis maintained their independence, although occasionally paying tribute to neighboring states.

Sometime during this three-hundred-year period Thull extended its boundaries over roughly 40 kilometers of river valley. Nomadic Gujars wrestled control of some pasture areas from neighboring Kohistani communities about this time, but were successfully repulsed from Thull. The strength of her fighting men allowed Thull to move the main village from its defensive site on a high plateau to a location closer to the river's edge. Then an earthquake, which shifted the course of the Panjkora to the east, created a propitious site for the new settlement, an old river terrace close to the valley's floor. Farmers could now exploit the rich bottom land at the river's edge.

By the mid-19th century powerful Yusufzai chiefs emerged in Southern Dir, who engaged in constant struggles for hegemony in the area. Alliances and oppositions shifted as ambitious men sought to further their aspirations at the expense of opponents. When the British formally established their rule over the plains of Malakand in 1849, a new player entered the game. Now struggles for supremacy among local leaders became small plays in a larger contest—the "great game" between the British and the Russians.

Dir, Swat, and Bajour concerned the British for two reasons: to ensure trade and commerce in the Empire and to protect India's northwest frontier. The rich farmlands of the Peshawar Valley (of which the plains of Malakand formed a part) added substantial wealth to British coffers. Yet trade, commerce, and profit required a modicum of tranquillity in order to flourish. Unfortunately for the Raj, the politically unsettled conditions in the mountains constantly threatened to spill onto the plains, disrupting peace and threatening revenue. To check this threat, British soldiers punished raids on her territory and disrespect for British authority by mounting punitive expeditions against the mountain tribesmen.

Tensions between England and Russia increased as the Russian Empire expanded in Central Asia to the northwest of India and the British Government became obsessed with protecting India's northwest border. Eventually the British incorporated into its sphere of influence first Kashmir, then Gilgit, and finally Chitral; protecting its influence in Chitral drew the British Government into active participation in the affairs of Dir. Frontier officers adopted a hands-off policy initially, interfering only minimally in the political affairs of the mountain tribes. Later, however, the British Government encouraged tribal chiefs to establish states, thereby bringing a semblance of order to the area. This policy ultimately led Umra Khan, a Pakhtun chief in southern Dir, to invade Kohistan in the late 19th century. The British armed his troops with modern rifles, and consequently he was able to defeat combined forces from Dir and Swat Kohistan. The Raj later drove Umra Khan into exile in Afghanistan, however, replacing him with a more politically sympathetic leader. Thull and her Kohistani neighbors nevertheless remained subject to Pakhtun rulers until the Pakistani Government abolished Dir as a state in the mid 1960s.

HEROES OF THE HINDU-KUSH

I suspect some who read this book will conclude that Kohistanis are bloodthirsty beasts—that their penchant for what seems to us chaotic violence makes them little more than wild animals. Thinking about Kohistanis this way, however, is a mistake with a long history in the West. It is a mistake, for it confines the peoples of the Hindu-Kush within the boundaries of Euro-American culture. Still the error is interesting, because it expresses hidden elements in our own cultural constructions of the world.

To understand why and how this is so, let us look in the unlikely corner of cardboard heroes. There we find Conan the Barbarian. In recent times Arnold Schwarzenegger made Conan famous by slaying the hordes of evil in two dismal Hollywood films. Conan originally hatched, however, in the mind of Robert Howard, an author of pulp fantasy who lived and wrote before World War II.

One Conan story, called "The People of the Black Circle," illustrates how Americans interpret violence (especially that of Hindu-Kush tribes) in a particularly revealing way. Set in the imaginary "Hyborian Age" sometime before the beginning of history, "The People of the Black Circle" records the exploits of Conan in the foothills of the "Himelian Mountains" on the "Northwest Frontier of Vendhya." Conan is the classic lone-wolf adventurer, generally unencumbered by kinship, community, or any other ties. Wandering from adventure to adventure, he fights, slaughters, plunders, and womanizes his way across the Hyborian continents. Although a kind of rough fairness orders Conan's actions toward others, he is basically lawless: a man who chafes under social rules, an outsider, a stranger.

As "The People of the Black Circle" begins, Conan has temporarily abandoned the life of solitary adventure to become chief of the Afghulis. Yet his relationship with his followers seems tenuous, based more on fear and avarice than loyalty and moral obligation. The Afghuli tribesmen follow Conan because of a grudging respect for his superior fighting ability and, even more importantly, because of lust for the plunder his leadership promises to provide. The relationship is one of calculation and self-interest on both sides. Leader and follower together value the other almost exclusively for what one can give the other. Thus, Conan tricks and ultimately abandons his followers, who turn on him in fury. In the end Conan flees the Himelian Mountains, once again the lone-wolf adventurer.

Obviously, much of the inspiration for "The People of the Black Circle" came from what Howard read about the tribes inhabiting the Hindu-Kush Mountains of eastern Afghanistan and the Northwest Frontier of India (now Pakistan). Such tribes as the "Wazulis," "Afghulis," "Irakzai," and "Dogozai" who appear in the story seem suspiciously similar to the Wazirs, Afridis, Orakzai, and Daudzai, tribes living along the border between Pakistan and Afghanistan.

In the genre of pulp fantasy the continuing success of the Conan stories is not surprising, for they express basic American notions about masculinity and heroism—notions most often contained in the archetypal American hero, the cowboy. As Elizabeth Lawrence explains in her analysis of rodeo culture, cowboys were men of rough manners, disdainful of routine, rebellious against the civilized world, and committed to a life of adventure in which it was not uncommon to ride away fast after a fight (1982:66–69)—a description closely resembling Conan.

Conan's resemblance to the cowboy hero should surprise no one, as Howard, the story's author, lived most of his life in Cross Plains, Texas. Just as important, the portrayal of Hindu-Kush tribesmen in the literature of Howard's time closely paralleled American ideas of cowboys as heroes. C. Collin Davies, writing in 1932 about the tribesmen of the Northwest Frontier, provides an excellent case in point:

> A rude, perfidious savage he may be, yet, one cannot but admire his proud bearing and resolute step, his martial instincts and independent spirit, his frank, open manners and festive temperament, his hatred of control, his love of country, and his wonderful powers of endurance. (1932:48)

Delete the word *perfidious* and Davies' description depicts not only the way many Americans conceptualize the cowboy hero but, indeed, the way Howard portrayed Conan.

Yet in the "People of the Black Circle" Conan and the Afghulis appear not so much as heroes in white hats, but more as heroic brigands—a Butch Cassidy and the hole-in-the-wall gang, raiding settlements and striking fear into the hearts of law-abiding citizens. Not surprisingly, the popular literature of Howard's time describes the people of the Hindu-Kush in a similar manner. For example, T. L. Pennell, a British missionary on the Northwest Frontier for many years, details a number of "outlaw" raids and attacks on "desperado" strongholds, while at the same time commenting on outlaw chiefs' sense of fair play (1913:17–30).

So then Howard used the Northwest Frontier Province of British India to situate "The People of the Black Circle," and in the story rewrote Hindu-Kush ethnography to express American beliefs about wild-west "hero/outlaws." Why is this significant? Is understanding how "The People of the Black Circle" emerged from the way Americans see the Sundance Kid only an arcane exercise in irrelevance? I think not, for it helps us understand how we sometimes make sense of people who institutionalize violence in their social relations. We use our own contrasting cultural categories (violence-prone cowboys versus peace-loving homesteaders) to put them in relief. From *Shane* to *The Magnificent Seven* to *The Outlaw—Josey Wales,* Hollywood beat to death this contrast between gunslingers and sodbusters. (In the process it taught us a morality of violence and celebrated the conquest and domination of the wild frontier by Western man.)

This raises the question, How does the way Americans think about gunslingers relate specifically to Howard's fantasies about Hindu-Kush tribes? Let us focus on his portrayal of the "natives" in the "The People of the Black Circle" for an answer. We need look no further than the following lines of the story.

Others pressed into the wavering circle of light—wild, ragged, bearded men, with eyes like wolves, and long blades in their fists. They did not see Yasmina, for she was hidden by Conan's massive body. But peeping from her covert, she knew icy fear for the first time that night. These men were more like wolves than human beings.

"What are you hunting in the Zhaibar by night, Yar Afzal? Conan demanded of the burly chief, who grinned like a bearded ghoul.

"Who knows what might come up the Pass after dark? We Wazulis are nighthawks. But what of you, Conan?" (1966:36)

Wazulis, then, are "wild, ragged, bearded men with eyes like wolves." They are, in fact, "more like wolves than human beings," although the Wazuli chief himself referred to his followers as "nighthawks."

Thus birds of prey and fierce carnivores, ferocious creatures who inhabit the realm of wild nature in our cultural scheme, provide the images for Howard's natives. These images make sense to us because we often understand male violence (including the violence of outlaw gunmen) as manifesting the dark, animal side of humanness. And we feel men's seemingly natural proclivity to violence must be tamed by culture, as settler women—ciphers for civilization—tamed Shane and Josey Wales. In taming violence, civilization can turn it against evil. Unsubdued, as Howard portrays the violence of Afghuli and Wazuli warriors, it is chaotic and hence bestial.

How can we evade what is in fact Howard's trap? How can we understand *dushmani* without the handcuffs of Western cultural categories? Anthropologists analyze vengeance from a number of theoretical perspectives, some escaping the trap better than others. The anthropological literature on organized vengeance is vast, and I can only sketch here a few of the more interesting perspectives. Readers interested in pursuing the anthropology of revenge in greater depth should start with "The Feud" in *The Anthropology of War: A Bibliography* (Ferguson and Farragher 1988).

One popular approach explains vengeance from a Darwinian perspective. Napoleon Chagnon, its chief proponent, argues that natural selection designs humans who make choices in terms of cost-benefit calculations. Moreover humans analyze alternatives in order to choose what maximizes reproductive advantages. Among the Yanomamo Indians of South America this generates blood feuding because taking vengeance both discourages would-be aggressors and increases men's sexual success with women. Thus feuding is rational behavior under certain conditions (and remember, natural selection designs humans who "naturally" make rational decisions) because it maximizes reproductive benefits (Chagnon 1988, 1989).

Chagnon's Darwinian theory of vengeance escapes the Conan trap in interesting ways. He does not propose that organized vengeance has rooted itself in our genes and therefore constitutes a part of human psychobiology. His argument is more subtle. Natural selection, he maintains, has "wired" us not so much for taking vengeance but more for making cost-benefit calculations. When seeking revenge is the most rational course of action, humans generally chose it over other alternatives, for that is our nature.

This is a powerful theory. Indeed, one can argue that natural selection favored organisms that solve problems more efficiently throughout the course of biological evolution. But those who swallow the Darwinian theory of vengeance too quickly should be wary, for it contains a poison pill.

At the end of his piece entitled "Life Histories, Blood Revenge, and Warfare in a Tribal Population" (1988), Chagnon describes a young Yanomamo sent by missionaries to the territorial capital, where he discovers a legal system that has made blood feuding obsolete and unnecessary. Taking vengeance in the city is murder in the Western sense and can either land one in court at best, or in jail at worst. Consequently, blood feuding makes sense as rational behavior maximizing reproduction only "under certain conditions," as Chagnon pointed out. For the Yanomamo "innocent" in the district capital, such "conditions" surely include the police, courts, judges, and politicians that make up sociopolitical institutions in nation-states.

Such institutions, however, form parts of sociocultural creations. Although biological evolution molded human nature—and human nature obviously effects the limits of our creations—we cannot reduce their structure and content to biology. This does not mean Darwinian theories of vengeance are wrong. On the contrary, they are right, but limited. Organized vengeance in Thull is, as we shall see, a cultural creation with complex rules and symbols thick with meaning. As an evolutionary mechanism shaping human biology, natural selection explains neither the peculiarities of such cultural creations nor the history of their development.

Chagnon's Darwinian theory of blood revenge centered on the "wiring" of rational choice into the human psyche through natural selection. Other blood feud theories build on this idea, but take it beyond biological evolution. Two of these mix rational choice with various forms of functionalism. Functional theory explains aspects of social and cultural systems by demonstrating that they help maintain a given sociocultural system or that they serve to answer fundamental human needs.

Following Evans-Pritchard's lead in *The Nuer* (1940), Jacob Black-Michaud argued in *Cohesive Force* that the primary function of feuds was to promote social cohesion in situations of scarce natural resources and rudimentary political organization. His analysis differed from standard functional explanations in its insistence on the role economic and political self-interest plays in feuding behavior. Black-Michaud saw feuds as transactional relationships based on calculated self-interest that are ultimately about "competition for leadership in situations in which egalitarian ideals and a lack of opportunities for economic differentiation prevail" (1975:25–26).

Christopher Boehm employed a different kind of functional perspective in *Blood Revenge* (1984). Whereas Black-Michaud analyzed feuds in relation to their function in maintaining systems of social relationships, Boehm took an ecological perspective, viewing social institutions or cultural traits in terms of their contribution to the survival or expansion of human populations within given environments. Much of *Blood Revenge* demonstrates how feuding institutions served to maintain a constant population in tribal Montenegro during the 19th century, where a mountain environment with scarce natural resources and an external predator in the Turkish Empire made survival problematic.

Like Chagnon and Black-Michaud, Boehm emphasized the importance of cost-benefit calculations for blood feud arrangements. He argued that the form feuding institutions take is a function of rational choices members of societies make in "containing or channeling homicidal violence" (1984:207). Social engineering involving cost-benefit calculations, therefore, determines the shape of feuding arrangements, and people design feud patterns to perform needed functions.

All functionalist perspectives are essentially teleological, that is, they explain parts of a sociocultural system by showing their consequences for some end or goal (Beattie 1964:52). Thus Black-Michaud saw institutions of the feud as interconnecting leadership patterns, forms of social organization, and values composing coherent wholes. The feud, in this view, defines a particular kind of social system. As long as it exists as a timeless institution the society exists as a timeless reality. Boehm, on the other hand, explained feuding arrangements as mechanisms of population stability; that is, they serve to maintain steady populations in given sociophysical environments.

The need for a different perspective is clear when we look at organized vengeance in Dir Kohistan. There blood feuding developed as the centerpiece of social organization only recently, and then alongside economic and political modernization. To understand blood feuding in Thull, therefore, we need a historical perspective, one that asks: What generates systems of organized vengeance?

Michael Meeker argued such an approach in "The Twilight of a South Asian Heroic Age" (1980), a reanalysis of Fredrik Barth's study of politics in Swat, the valley adjacent to Dir in the east. Meeker's general point is that political arrangements in Swat can best be understood as resulting from historical processes rather than the workings of a relatively timeless sociocultural system. Specifically the conquest of the Swatis, an agrarian population native to the valley, by the heroic Yusufzai tribe in the 16th century was decisive for the future of Swat society. Since then, the tension between a concern for communal harmony—a feature of agrarian societies—and the obsession with individual advantage and fascination with personal honor, glory, and violence—the dark side of heroic societies—has shaped social relations in the valley. In other words, social interaction in Swat came to be distorted by a strain between valuing the use of coercive force and honoring diligent labor and peaceful cooperation (1980:697).

"The Twilight of a South Asian Heroic Age" is a fascinating analysis, skillfully constructed and subtly argued. Yet Conan nags at me whenever I read it, for the way Meeker thought about heroic societies bears a striking resemblance to Howard's portrayal of Conan and his Afghuli followers, as the following lines show.

> Heroic identity turns upon *personal* strategies and *personal* [emphasis Meeker's] instruments devoted to force and coercion. That is to say, there is an individualistic dimension to the hero who is often specifically associated with the disruption of polity, society and even family. As an ideal in folk epics, he was a member

of a small band of adventurers whose very way of life involved extortion, kidnapping, raiding and pillaging. And, in fact, such companions in adventure were often to be found on the margins of polity and society, uprooted from their homelands and separated from their families. (1980:682–683)

One might almost believe Meeker had Conan specifically in mind when he wrote this passage.

The uncanny fit between Conan and the Afghulis and Meeker's heroic Ysufzai raises unsettling questions. If Meeker's agrarian/heroic contrast is ultimately rooted in American culture, it may camouflage as much as illuminate the peoples of the Hindu-Kush. On the surface Conan, the Afghulis, and the Yusufzai may resemble Butch Cassidy and the hole-in-the-wall gang, and the autochthonous Swati farmers may favor Nebraska sodbusters, but superficial similarities can obscure more profound differences.

This is not to say that Meeker was wrong to focus on violence and personal strategy in the Swat Valley. But, making agrarian and heroic into types of societies may distort these features as much as clarify them. We need to delve deeper into the history and ethnography of the Hindu-Kush to better understand violence and personal strategy as they operate there.

Let us return for a moment to Meeker's interpretation of Hindu-Kush history to develop the argument a bit further. According to Meeker:

the Pakhtun (that is, Yusufzai) conquest was only the last of many similar invasions, the record of which extends back into the archaic period. That is to say, the agrarian societies in this part of the Old World had to take shape under the circumstances of repeated conquests by heroic tribes which, for centuries, perhaps for millennia, competed with one another over the right to dominate various agrarian societies that were reduced to the status of subject peoples. (1980:687)

Hindu-Kush history, according to this view, records waves of conquests in which heroic peoples replaced one another as rulers over agrarian people. A close look at the historical record, however, shows a greater complexity. We can generally classify conquest cases in the Hindu-Kush as follows:

1. Invaders conquer and subsequently rule over defeated populations, only to be conquered in turn by fresh waves of invaders. Meeker maintains that this is the general pattern in the area, and both Swat and Chitral seem to exemplify it. In Chitral, to the northwest of Swat, Kalash invaders from what is now Afghanistan defeated and subjugated the local population, only to be vanquished and subjugated themselves by succeeding invaders several centuries later. Interestingly enough, however, in the Chitral case "heroic" peoples did not so much replace one another as rulers over an "agrarian" population. On the contrary, "heroic" invaders defeated "heroic" defenders (themselves the "heroic" invaders of an earlier era), who henceforth became the subjugated "agrarian" population. Actually, the situation in Chitral was even more complex. In the main Chitral valleys the Kalash did suffer defeat and subjugation. However, some Kalash retreated to a few remote valleys where they maintained political control over local affairs, although forced to pay tribute to their conquerors.

2. Conquering peoples drive out vanquished populations, expropriating their land in the process. Conquerors do not rule the conquered communities as a subject population. For example, invaders defeated in battle and subsequently expelled populations in Rashung in Swat, the Waigul Valley in Nuristan, and the Panjkora Valley in the immediate vicinity of Dir town.
3. People inhabiting high mountain valleys with effective natural defenses repel invaders and maintain varying degrees of political independence. This situation was most common in the Hindu-Kush region. The various Nuristani, Kohistani, and Pashai tribal communities (with a total population exceeding a half a million people) exemplify variations on this general pattern.

The third case is particularly interesting because it represents the most common pattern in the region, and at the same time appears to support the heroic/agrarian contrast, if not Meeker's historical interpretation of it. Among the "fortress" tribes of the Hindu-Kush, maintaining communal harmony is (or at least was until very recently) a highly effective value in ordering politics within communities. Among the Yusufzai and other Pakhtun invaders, in contrast, institutionalized violence and complex notions of personal honor organized (and in most cases still organize) significant aspects of intracommunity relations.

Whether or not Meeker's heroic/agrarian concepts are useful in distinguishing types of Hindu-Kush societies, he did identify an important issue in Hindu-Kush ethnography: How can we explain the difference between communities in which intercommunity violence is endemic and those societies are obsessed with communal harmony? Moreover, he pointed to a solution by encouraging us to take a historical perspective—to analyze the historical circumstances conditioning the contexts in which patterns of social interaction unfold. He persuasively argued that power relationships in Swat must be understood as existing within, and affected by, fields of tensions influenced by historical events.

For Meeker, the tensions between individual glory and violence, and cooperation and communal harmony that define political contexts in Swat are residues of history, resulting from the conquest of peace-loving, agrarian people by heroic societies. Placing his analysis in a wider ethnographic/historical context, however, suggests an alternative interpretation. The tension between valuing violence and individual glory, and prizing cooperation and communal harmony distinguishes cultural systems in most, if not all, Hindu-Kush communities through time. But the degree to which one or the other set of principles commands center stage and the way in which social relations institutionalize them vary in response to the course of history.

Meeker may have been caught in the Conan trap, but he also pointed to the best escape, especially in thinking about violence in Hindu-Kush societies like Thull, for he focused attention on the forces effecting change in the tense interplay between communal harmony and intracommunity violence. The following pages try to understand blood feud violence in Thull from this perspective. First we learn how institutionalized vengeance came to dominate social relationships, which involves examining how historical changes in religious ideology and political economy transformed violence in the community. Once transformed, blood feud violence in turn influenced social arrangements; consequently, we also study how death enmity affected economic, kinship, and political organization. The book, therefore, falls into two parts, focusing first on the forces generating death enmity, and then on its consequences. The concluding chapter, based on my personal journal, discusses the fieldwork itself and places the research in perspective, showing how my peculiar experiences affected my understanding of Thull and structured my account.

2 / The Course of the Feud

The long bus ride from Thull to Dir town is a torment, made worse by dust and a rutted dirt track passing for a road. The bus itself quickly fills to capacity with passengers. Those who cannot cram into the seats either hang precariously off the back, or climb on top, crowding within the intricate metal rack that surrounds the bus's roof. Although adorned with garish scenes of speeding streamliners and modern F-15 fighter planes, the bus would agonize over the boulders and ditches littering the road, a remnant of the past, ancient even by Pakistani standards. Always, then, when I made my biweekly grocery run to the market in Dir town, friends or acquaintances would beg to come. Though my jeep could not comfortably accommodate all would-be riders, usually most people somehow jammed into the back seat. Their various contortions never ceased to amaze me.

The bus to Dir

One trip particularly etched itself in my memory. For three years Anwar, my good friend and informant, sought vengeance for his brother's murder. He carefully hoarded his money until finally he possessed enough to buy the rifle that would permit him to kill his enemy. I agreed to take him as far as Dir town. There he could catch a bus to Bajour, where local gun shops sold good-quality firearms. I also promised a place in the jeep to Mir Said, who each night slept outside my door with his rifle, guarding my safety. Moments before we left, Mir Said's brother-in-law Qai Afsal sauntered up, his Russian-made automatic assault rifle slung across his shoulder. Mir Said immediately hugged the door, and Qai Afsal crowded in. Tension, as well as people, filled the jeep.

Anwar's close friendship with Golam Sarwar, one of Qai Afsal's enemies, caused the strained atmosphere. *Mar dushmani* ("death enmity") did not formally organize social relations between Anwar and Qai Afsal. Still, everyone in the community recognized the potential for violence between them. Most of the time the two men avoided one another with studied carelessness.

But much to my surprise, the tension in the jeep quickly dissipated. Throughout the five-hour trip to Dir town Qai Afsal and Anwar laughed, joked, and gossiped together. Even more astonishing, they swore everlasting friendship, referring to each other as *ja* ("brothers"). Later I asked Anwar if he and Qai Afsal felt as friendly toward one another as they had acted in the jeep. Anwar thought a minute, then said, "*Doske dos, radke dushman.*" The words translate, "friend by day, enemy by night"; they capture an essential dimension of organized vengeance in Thull.

THE CULTURE OF SOCIAL RELATIONS

The people of Thull think about the quality of social relations in terms of contrasting concepts. Of these, enmity/amity, bad/good, enemy/ally, and distrust/suspicion/trust most typify how people think about *dushmani*. For example, bad (*lal*) relations, manifested by distrust and hostility, characterize the ties existing between enemies (*dushmans*). *Tani* ("allies"), in contrast, have good (*ran*) relations; amity and trust order their relationships. Exchanging bullets and blows (with fist, axe, knife, or club) whenever possible and refusing either to give or accept food and drink express enmity. Sharing personal possessions and sustenance and exchanging labor indicate amity and trust.

Most men in Thull interact neither as allies nor enemies. In some instances they relate as *maxilaf* ("opponents"). *Roshagat* (roughly "anger") defines such relationships, and whereas physical assault expresses *roshagat*, murder does not. *Maxilafs*, like *dushmans*, never eat together and in general attempt to weaken one another whenever possible. How men in Thull usually acted toward the government veterinarian during his visits to vaccinate livestock illustrates the point. The veterinarian did not realize the opportunities he offered for expressing anger toward opponents. Thus the first man the veterinarian saw always attempted to cloak his arrival in secrecy so that his opponents could not benefit from the veterinarian's services. He would spirit the veterinarian away to his guest room before anyone else knew of his arrival in town. The host would then ply him with ever-increasing amounts of food and drink to keep him safely cloistered. This tactic made sense to my friend Anwar, for as he explained, "By hiding the veterinarian I keep my *maxilaf*'s animals sick."

A man possesses more ambiguous relations with the opponents of his allies. Technically, bad relations do not exist between them. The wise man, however, always stays wary of such men, for they can become dangerous adversaries at any time. Finally, most men in Thull connect as community members only. In some ways, these relationships pose the greatest danger because of their fluidity—they can unexpectedly change to relationships of alliance or enmity at any moment. As a result neither trust nor distrust but guarded suspicion structures behavior between most men in Thull, and for good reason. As Anwar explained, smiling words express normal good manners, but only fools trust those who speak them. "Masters of deceit" is how the men of Thull describe themselves; hence, those who give smiles during the day may well give bullets at night.

To make his point, Anwar told me how his brother, Said Omar, died. Said Omar lived in the Kallan section of Thull, an area at the foot of the mountains on Thull's eastern border. Unlike Thull Proper, houses in Kallan are scattered among fields and pastures. One day Said Omar heard via village gossip that his neighbor Dilawar Khan had nothing left to eat. Though Said Omar did not have close relations with Dilawar Khan, he assumed Dilawar Khan harbored no feelings of enmity toward him. So gathering a basket of bread and cheese, he proceeded to Dilawar Khan's house, located about a hundred yards away, and knocked on the door. This was a fatal mistake, for when it opened Dilawar Khan stood in the doorway, his rifle at his shoulder. Dilawar Khan fired immediately, the bullet going straight through Said Omar's heart, killing him instantly. Adding insult to murder, Dilawar Khan unleashed his attack dogs when Said Omar's young son attempted to retrieve his father's body.

"But why", I asked, "would a man kill his neighbor who only tried to help him?"

"Who knows?" Anwar shrugged, "The night gave him death. But I will take vengeance."

I did not doubt him.

Other men explained similar events to me. One evening Golam Sarwar invited his friend Fakir to share a meal at his house. About nine o'clock, after a pleasant evening of good food and gossip, Fakir left to return home. As far as anyone knew Fakir had no death enemies. Yet, about ten minutes later hidden assailants sprang an ambush and Fakir lay dead, shot in the head by unknown enemies. The next morning five men, neighbors of Fakir, left the village for the high mountain pastures. Although they admitted guilt by their actions, they never publicly acknowledged committing the murder and never gave any reason for killing Fakir.

Golam Sarwar explained it similarly: "The night killed him." And, he, like Anwar, swore vengeance. No one doubted his word either, for soon he purchased an expensive Russian AK-47 assault rifle to use against his enemies. The five putative murderers fled to Kallan, where they built a house/fortress for their defense. They enjoyed only limited success. No one has died as yet, but in surprise ambushes hidden assailants seriously wounded two men closely related to the supposed murderers. Nevertheless, until the enemies formally conclude peace arrangements, violence will continue. Enemies did murder Fakir at night, but to say the night killed him only means that no one knows the real reason. Men don't kill without cause, though, and everyone in Thull understands the grounds for homicide. We will return to the reasons why men kill one another, but first more about secrecy.

Competition pervades Thull, and anyone not an ally is at least a potential rival. Men expect duplicity from rivals and believe success, if not survival, often hinges on uncovering the secrets of others. At the same time, successful men keep their own affairs as confidential as possible. Because social standing is vulnerable to gossip, the more one knows about the private affairs of enemies and rivals, the easier to attack them through malicious talk. From an early age parents encourage children to hone their skills at collecting information, for the people of Thull consider intelligence gathering high art.

DEATH ENMITY

So far I have outlined several general features of social relations in Thull important for understanding *mar dushmani*. Now I will focus more on death enmity itself. As a general principle men should retaliate whenever another wrongs them, though the act of revenge itself should not exceed the original wrong. A blow should answer a blow and a death answer a death. Conversely, attacks on men through wives, sisters, and daughters usually require deadly violence; killing the offender is the most appropriate response. For example, staring at a man's wife, daughter, or sister (if she is of marriageable age) demands the offender's death. Thus, according to some gossips, Dilawar Khan killed Anwar's brother, Said Omar, because he came to stare at Dilawar Khan's wife. Said Omar, they said, brought the basket of food as a cynical ploy to deceive his neighbor.

Vengeance, therefore, structures two kinds of relationships. In the first, *maxilaf*s share anger (*roshagat*), and the aggrieved tries to injure his opponent. In the second, *dushman*s share death enmity (*mar dushmani*), and the aggrieved tries to kill his enemy. Yet the rules do not always require taking revenge. In cases of physical injury and murder, the wronged party can choose to settle the case peacefully by accepting compensation. Attacks through women, by comparison, usually require deadly retaliation.

A dushman *prepared for his enemies*

Enemies can peacefully settle *mar dushmani* in two ways. First, if the murderer feels desperate for fear his *dushman* will kill him, then he can sue for peace. Even so, asking for mercy requires taking risks. The murderer must enter his enemy's guest room holding his dagger with a piece of white cloth tied to its blade. If he enters before his enemy kills him, then he must crawl under one of the string beds in the room. He calls out from there, "Kill me! I am at your mercy."

The man suing for peace is not asking his *dushman* to kill him but formally requesting he accept compensation instead of seeking revenge. An enemy cannot kill such a foe while the man is in his house. Nevertheless the rules do not require he abandon vengeance. If he refuses to forego revenge, then he must find a close relative to eject the enemy from his house. He will usually say to his kinsman, "A dog is in my house! Make him leave!"

Informants claimed that *dushman*s often ask for mercy in this manner. No one criticizes those who do, because suing for peace does not make one *baghrairat* ("without honor"). Yet no one settled *dushmani* in this manner while I lived in Thull. Apparently enemies more normally make peace at community meetings called by influential politicians. Respected leaders unrelated to either side entreat vengeance-seekers to accept compensation. Technically a vengeance-seeker can accept or reject such pleas. Even so, he will most likely acquiesce if those of high standing among his allies pressure him to do so.

Men usually pay compensation for murder in money, normally a sum of four to six thousand dollars. Sometimes they give land, and more rarely women in marriage. After the opposing sides agree to the compensation, the former enemies share a ritual meal of rice and meat. At its close, a *mullana* (religious scholar/leader) intones a special prayer, and the bad relations between the two *dushmans* theoretically end. The murdered man's father, sons, and brothers usually divide the compensation. Sometimes paternal uncles and cousins also take shares. This occurs, however, only when they have actively sought revenge (possibly because the murdered man possessed no adult brothers or sons, and a father too old to seek vengeance). Men prefer to avenge themselves on the murderer himself, but Kohistanis believe that killing a father, adult brother, or adult son also evens the score. Killing any other kinsman is inappropriate, while killing women and children is unheard of.

Paying compensation does not always terminate *dushmani*. The possibility always exists that someone will seek vengeance even after a blood feud has been peacefully settled. Vengeance often involves the enmity of many people, and not all allies share in the compensation. A friend or distant relative who feels aggrieved, but not recompensed by compensation, sometimes takes it upon himself to seek vengeance in spite of the settlement. Moreover, men often relax their vigilance after paying compensation. Thus vengeance-seekers sometimes agree to peace as a ploy to trick enemies into lowering their guard, making them easier to kill. One cannot commit such revenge murders openly, though, because taking vengeance after the ritual meal formerly ending *dushmani* violates community morality. At the same time, to demonstrate their honor, such vengeance-takers usually find a way to make their deed an open secret in the community.

QAI AFSAL'S *DUSHMANI*

So far we have looked at some of the more important general features of organized vengeance in Thull, but specific cases often manifest general features in peculiar ways. To better grasp how organized violence works, I turn to a particularly interesting case involving instances of violence occurring over a five-year period. It began, innocently enough, one afternoon in the summer of 1979. Mamad Said, Ramadin, and Amin spent the day together in the mountains herding their goats. Ramadin joked about Amin's prowess as a hunter, and Amin playfully shoved Ramadin in return. Mamad Said, getting into the spirit of things, picked up a stick and swung it at Amin in mock seriousness, intending to miss. Unfortunately, at that precise moment Amin turned toward Mamad Said, catching the blow directly across the face. Blood began to flow, and the afternoon turned ugly. Amin staggered to a lean-to in a nearby pasture where his maternal uncle, Shah Hajji Khan, and several cousins herded their goats.

Shah Hajji Khan and Mamad Said shared membership in the same patrilineage, the Hasanor, although Mamad Said belonged to the Piror segment, whereas Shah Hajji Khan was a *malik* ("man of influence" or "leader") in the Paiyapor (see Figure 1). Amin belonged to a different patrilineage altogether. Even so, Shah Hajji Khan supported Amin, his sister's son, because men often share strong bonds with their maternal relatives. The next day Amin, his uncle Hajji, and several cousins attacked Mamad Said's lean-to. They hoped to catch him unawares and inflict an injury similar to the one suffered by Amin. Several of Mamad Said's paternal cousins camped nearby raced to the scene upon hearing his cries for help. They brought axes, spades, and fighting clubs to the melee. The battle left many seriously wounded, but Amin and his supporters had by far the worst of the fight. Shah Hajji Khan's own son suffered broken bones, and an axe blow to the head almost ended his life.

Because of the injuries suffered, the men involved became *maxilaf*s ("formal opponents"). Because no one died, anger (*roshagat*) rather than death enmity (*mar dushmani*) defined the nature of their opposition. Shah Hajji Khan craved vengeance for the wounds suffered by his son, but an injury equal to them rather than death would suffice to avenge them. To this end he asked help from Khan Akbar, an uninvolved third person but also a member of the Hasanor. In return Shah Hajji Khan formally joined Khan Akbar's political party.

THE HASANOR

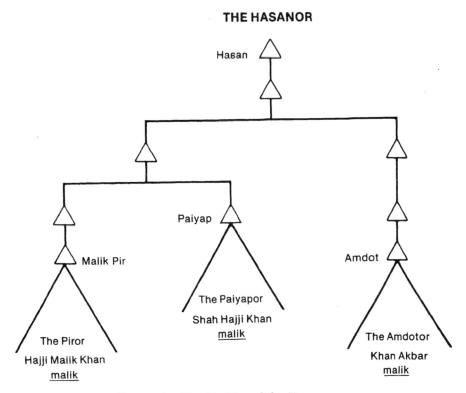

Figure 1   The Maliks of the Hasanor

A brief outline of the Hasanor's internal organization will help in understanding how the case developed (see Figure 1). Three segments of closely related paternal kin subdivide the group: the Amdotor, descended from Amdot, the Paiyapor, descended from Paiyap, and the Piror, descended from Malik Pir. One man stands out as the most important leader (*malik*) in each segment. Khan Akbar is *malik* of the Amdotor segment, Shah Hajji Khan the *malik* of the Paiyapor, and Hajji Malik Khan the *malik* of the Piror. The Paiyapor share a closer relationship with the Piror than the Amdotor. Consequently, Shah Hajji Khan usually supported Hajji Malik Khan against Khan Akbar when the two opposed one another in political competition. However, the fight that began as innocent play in the Hasanor pastures changed the previous arrangements forever.

When Shah Hajji Khan gave his formal support to Khan Akbar, the opposition between Hajji Malik Khan and Khan Akbar significantly intensified. Interestingly enough, the original incident, in which Mamad Said reorganized Amin's face, lost its importance. Two years later, when Mamad Said died from tuberculosis, Amin's interest in taking vengeance ceased. Now the dispute centered on the unavenged injury suffered by Shah Hajji Khan's son during the wild melee in the Hasanor pastures. His longing for revenge intensified the already bitter rivalry between Khan Akbar and Hajji Malik Khan.

One might think that the individual fights, group ambushes, and melees of the Hasanor expressed descent group rivalries, but appearances deceive. The rivalry between Khan Akbar and Hajji Malik Khan exemplifies what people call *dalabasi,* a rivalry pitting *dalas* ("factions," "blocks," or perhaps better, "parties") against one another, rather than descent groups. When third-party mediators fail to convince protagonists to settle their differences peacefully, confrontations escalate in their intensity. As each side gathers its allies, *dalas* emerge to confront one another.

Originally, intense, even dangerous *dalabasi* opposed Hajji Malik Khan and Khan Akbar, but the rivalry was not deadly. That changed in the next few years. In the spring of 1982 Khan Akbar and Shah Hajji Khan hatched their plot to ambush Mamad Said. The opportunity to avenge the wounds suffered by his son had finally come within Shah Hajji Khan's reach. But the ambush failed. Mamad Said escaped by hiding in an irrigation ditch, and a few months later he died of tuberculosis. No one blamed his death on the failed ambush—no one, that is, except Mamad Said's brother, Qai Afsal.

Qai Afsal stands out in a crowd. He had had a bad reputation as a teenager, many in Thull calling him a *badmash* (a "looter," an "outlaw"— a kind of Kohistani Hell's Angel). According to his friend Gul Mir, Qai Afsal finally gave up stealing for a more respectable avocation in Thull, *dushmani.* Still he remained proud of his reputation as a "bad dude." The swagger in his walk, the hat cocked low over one eye, the twirling of his long luxurious mustache, the casual but practiced handling of his Kalashnikov assault rifle all convey the image of a dangerous man. Many men in Thull find him cocksure and abrasive.

In his heart Qai Afsal never accepted that tuberculosis had precipitated his brother's death. Instead he believed that the cold water of the irrigation ditch had caused him to die. Qai Afsal's opportunity for revenge came the following year during *Ramazan,* the month of fasting. One day, Khan Akbar sent his son, a man named Sakhi, to the high mountain pastures to oversee the family's numerous goats and cattle. After dark, while he hunted for a secluded spot to urinate, a hidden assailant shot him down in a hail of automatic rifle fire. Qai Afsal dropped from sight for a week. Even though no one saw him pull the trigger, everyone knew he was the killer. Because he did not deny killing Sakhi and because he disappeared immediately after the murder, Qai Afsal proved his guilt beyond a doubt to Khan Akbar, who immediately began plotting revenge.

Qai Afsal's alleged assassination of Sakhi notably changed social relations in several ways. The focus of Khan Akbar's *dalabasi* shifted from Hajji Malik Khan to Qai Afsal. More importantly, its nature changed from *roshagat* to *mar dushmani* (from "anger" to "death enmity"). Khan Akbar made his first move a few months later. Qai Afsal and his friend Ramadine secretly planned a trip to the bazaar in Kalkot, a neighboring Kohistani community. Unknown to Qai Afsal, spies discovered the plans in time for Khan Akbar to lay an ambush along the road to Kalkot. As Qai Afsal and his friend returned to Thull, a volley of bullets cut down Ramadine. Miraculously Qai Afsal walked into the village unscathed.

The murder of Ramadine should have created a new relationship of *dushmani* between Khan Akbar and Ramadine's close relatives. But Ramadine's kin abrogated their responsibility because they were too poor and too few to take vengeance. By their act they became *baghrairatman*s ("individuals with no character, no self-respect, no honor"). Ramadine's father publicly declared that Qai Afsal himself should decide whether to seek revenge.

By refusing to avenge his murder, Ramadine's kin further complicated the enmity between Khan Akbar and Qai Afsal and made it more difficult to settle matters peacefully. Now Qai Afsal and Khan Akbar each owed the other murder. Again Khan Akbar made the first move. One morning in the summer of 1984, Qai Afsal left my house after exchanging gossip and requesting medicine for his wife's illness. When he reached the road, rifle shots rang from Khan Akbar's property located on the high mesa dominating the road. The bullets hit close to his feet, but Qai Afsal sauntered down the road with his usual swagger. He did not even look in the direction from which the shots came.

Six days later his luck almost ran out. At seven fifteen that evening rifle bullets struck Qai Afsal in the arm and stomach as he left his house. Although badly wounded, he somehow managed to crawl back through his front door and return fire with his Kalashnikov machine gun. His close paternal kin who lived nearby quickly opened fire on his attackers. The battle raged about thirty minutes before third-party elders intervened to stop the fighting. Dilawar Sher (always the consummate politician looking to put people in his debt) took Qai Afsal to a government hospital in Peshawar, where major surgery saved his life.

Serious fighting broke out again two weeks later. A member of Khan Akbar's faction hid in a tree close to Qai Afsal's house in hopes of gathering some useful intelligence. But one of Qai Afsal's paternal cousins discovered the intruder's presence and blazed away with his rifle. The bullets missed, allowing the spy to scramble down the tree and sprint to his uncle's house, located a few hundred yards away. The uncle returned fire, and others on both sides joined the fight.

Two miles away Khan Akbar heard the shooting; gathering his allies, he hurried to the scene of battle. In a surprise move Golam Sarwar and his paternal kin entered the fighting on the side of Khan Akbar. Later I learned that Golam Sarwar had met secretly with Khan Akbar a few days earlier, and had agreed to become his ally. He did so for a number of reasons. First, a close friend was a member of Khan Akbar's *dala*. Second, Khan Akbar had promised to help in Golman Sarwar's *dushmani* with the killers of Fakir. Golam Sarwar and Khan Akbar shared distant kinship, because Khan Akbar had married Golam Sarwar's maternal cousin. Finally, Golam Sarwar disliked Qai Afsal, a reason as significant as any other for him to ally with Said Omar.

The fire fight lasted about three hours, until well after dark. Tracers lit the sky as bullets flew in all directions. Although outnumbered, Qai Afsal's *dala* successfully withstood their attackers, because they possessed greater fire power. Finally, onlookers in Thull had had enough. Several prominent leaders representing powerful groups of allies walked between the warring parties, forcing them to stop fighting. Miraculously, neither side scored any hits, whether by design or poor marksmanship I will never know.

The intensity of the fighting and the number of people involved on each side worried many people in Thull, even though no one was killed. Qai Afsal's *dushmani* with Khan Akbar appeared out of control, threatening many uninvolved members of the community. The same leaders who intervened to stop the battle called a meeting of all the adult men in the community. They hoped to cajole the opposing sides to make peace. Qai Afsal refused to attend, so the attempt fizzled. Nonetheless, the leaders made their point. Temporarily, at least, both sides refrained from further violence. When I left Thull, however, real peace between Qai Afsal and Khan Akbar seemed only a distant possibility.

The significance of Qai Afsal's case lies in what it teaches about the source of *dushmani*'s power in Thull. As his close friend Gul Mir said, Qai Afsal and he bullied their peers and scandalized their elders as teenegers. Both, however, stopped behaving immorally when they became men and pious Muslims. His own piety, Gul Mir said, expresses itself through participation in the activities of a pan-Islamic brotherhood, while Qai Afsal's piety expresses itself in *dushmani*.

That anyone could believe *dushmani* constitutes religious piety shocked my research assistant, Shahid Mahmood, a Punjabi from eastern Pakistan and a man well versed in orthodox Islam. Shahid's grandfather was a respected religious scholar in Rawalpindi before his death, and Shahid was raised studying Islamic theology. He knew that Islam does not advocate violence and that most Muslims do not countenance murder. Yet many men from Thull argue that taking vengeance is a religious act. Understanding the wellsprings of *dushmani*, therefore, requires examining Thull's peculiar version of Islamic ideology. Accordingly we turn in the next chapter to religious beliefs in Thull and how they empower blood feuding.

3 / The Power of Islam

A Kohistani mosque

Visitors to Thull see mosques everywhere they look. I counted eighteen but was never certain I had found them all. They range from simple wooden platforms scattered along the road and next to the river, to ornately decorated buildings situated at the center of settlement clusters. In the plains beneath the Malakand Pass villagers construct concrete mosques, but in Kohistan men build mosques primarily of wood and stone. The roof of the community's central mosque, located in the core settlement (called "Thull Proper," using a borrowed English word), rests on gigantic wood columns covered with carved geometric figures of fantastic design.

From the central mosque one can easily find the low one-story house, whose considerable size distinguishes it from its neighbors. In this building resides one of the most influential religious leaders in Thull, a learned Muslim scholar who teaches Islamic faith in the local primary school. He wields considerable power in community affairs because of his reputation for religious learning and piety. The building's large, flat roof, called *torwalo shan* ("Torwal's roof") after its original builder, provides a site for town meetings and is a constant reminder of the political vigor of Islam. Indeed Islam lies over, under, in front of, behind, around, and beyond society and culture in Thull; nothing escapes its sway.

I first saw *torwalo shan* during my initial visit to Thull, when I attended a town council (*jirga*), an unforgettable experience, to say the least. Dilaram Sher and Gul Shah, two important town leaders, called the meeting to decide whether I could reside in the community. Both men stand out because of their openness to contacts with the outside world. Dilaram Sher's lucrative timber business requires that he develop and maintain relations with government bureaucrats. Frequent business trips outside Thull gave him a taste for cosmopolitan ideas and imported consumer goods. He once appeared at my door, sporting an AK-47 assault rifle, a fishing rod, a camera, a bandolier of bullets, and a thermos jug with the smile logo and English motto "Have a Happy Day" printed on its front. Gul Shah's reputation comes from his learning, intelligence, reputation for religious piety, and his wealth. He continually searches for ways to tear down barriers and in the process open Thull to the wider pan-Islamic community. Both men are "progressives" in their own way, dedicated to changing Thull; both sponsored me because of their connections to my government sponsors outside the community.

Over four hundred men attended, most squatting on their haunches (with their heels flat to the ground) in rows lined on three sides of the roof. Gul Shah and Dilaram Sher led my research assistant, Shahid Mahmood, and me to a row of chairs facing the crowd. No one smiled, at least no one I could see, many scowled, and some even spat on the ground in my general direction. I was unnerved to say the least, feeling like a lost sheep in a wolf pack. From that inauspicious beginning, events rapidly proceeded downhill. Dilaram Sher's short opening speech preceded Gul Shah's more lengthy oration. Later I learned that Dilaram Sher had introduced my request, whereas Gul Shah had argued its merits. As my friend Anwar explained, "Dilaram Sher shot his rifle from Gul Shah's shoulder." The meeting then opened to general debate. Only grey-bearded men of haughty demeanor spoke. Although I understood no Kohistani at the time, their harsh, bellicose voices and cruel-looking eyes conveyed a world of meaning. I was not surprised, therefore, when Gul Shah turned and said to my assistant in Urdu, "They oppose us. The elders say we should never allow foreigners to live in Thull. *Kafir* (roughly, "infidel") foreigners cannot be trusted. He should not stay."

Shahid, my research assistant, slowly rose to face the crowd and, with his head bowed and his hands outstretched, began to recite the *Kalima,* the Muslim witness to faith. The angry muttering hushed as the beautiful tones of his almost musical chant transformed the moment. When the last words of the sacred text died away, "*Allah Akbar! Allah Akbar! Allah Akbar!*" ("God is great! God is great! God is great!") quietly resonated through the gathering.

The tones of voice, expressions of emotion, and body postures appropriate to political debate suddenly became unsuitable, indeed unacceptable. The *Kalima* demanded a new propriety.

A moment of silence passed, and then Shahid began speaking to the gathering in Urdu; Gul Shah translated his words into Kohistani for the benefit of the old men who could not understand. Political oratory constitutes high art in South Asia and Shahid mastered the craft long ago during his days as a student politician. He took the style of extemporaneous speech developed by Muslim fundamentalist preachers as the model for his creation, clothing our request in religion. After introducing each of us, he briefly explained that I wished to study the history and customs of the community. Then he began to construct his major theme, that our living in the village would strengthen Islam. Initially he talked about personal safety. We feared nothing, he said, for our fate, as everyone's fate, lies in the hands of God. Fate determines life and death, but our honor depends on how we revere God, and respecting God protects our honor. So whether we live or die means nothing. No government, no weapons, no human authority can provide true sanctuary, for one finds that only within God. But we also feared nothing because the people of Thull had a superb reputation for Muslim piety and hospitality. We wished to live in Thull precisely because of the piety of its people, since it made them excellent teachers of religion. Moreover, our learning about Islam would strengthen it. Although others had asked us to live with them, we could learn more about religion in Thull. Finally, the people of Thull would collect God's reward if our living in their community actually strengthened Islam.

Shahid's words ended. After a moment of silence first one, then another, then another, and finally every man attending the meeting waved their hands in unison. Gul Shah leaned toward us and, with a dazed look on his face, said the council had decided we could live in Thull. The clerk for the District Commissioner accompanying us shook his head in disbelief. The men of Thull, he told us, almost never agree to any proposal from outside the community.

The effect of Shahid's speech dramatically introduced me to the power of Islam in Kohistani social relations. Contrary to Shahid's words, most people throughout the Northwest Frontier believe Kohistanis are savages. They judge them as rude barbarians who only recently converted to Islam and practice its tenets poorly at best. The people of Thull know how neighboring ethnic groups judge them. Yet the roots of Kohistani sense of self lie in Muslim identity, and Thull men obsess over demonstrating their Muslim piety. Shahid's speech forced them into a corner with its subtle but clear subtext—namely, everyone knows Muslims have a duty to convert Kafirs to Islam. I wished to live in Thull to learn about Islam. Teaching me Islam would provide an excellent opportunity to convert me. Therefore refusing my request meant refusing to take seriously the responsibility to convert Kafirs and would reconfirm that the people of Thull practice their religion only half-heartedly at best, as their neighbors claimed. Almost the entire male population adamantly opposed my staying in town for more than a short time (and the shorter the better). Yet they could publicly admit to a superficial commitment to Islam only at great personal cost. Shahid had struck at the community's poor reputation for religious piety and subtly played both on their need for others to see them, and their need to see themselves, as good, pious Muslims. Thus I became the first Kafir ever to live in Thull for more than ten days. Unfortunately, in spite of Shahid's best efforts, most people continued to dislike and distrust me. Many never stopped thinking I secretly intended to steal their forest, and some always called me *kafrot*—which stands in relation to Kafir as "spic" stands to Hispanic, and "nigger" stands to Negro. From the beginning I knew I would never make it to honorary-member-of-the-tribe status.

Who cares, though, if anthropologists get ulcers doing research in Thull? And whether religious fanaticism reigns supreme in Kohistan depends on one's perspective. However, looking at my experiences in entering the community makes it easier to understand the impact of Islam on social relations. More to the point, they help us understand its power in shaping death enmity. Although formulated as cultural rules for behavior, Thull's version of Islamic ideology does not determine what its people do in any mechanical fashion. Instead Islam possesses the power to distort action—to bend, twist, unshape, and reshape it. In many instances Islam culturally defines meaningful options. Sometimes it weights these differently so that people pay prices and obtain rewards for choosing to act in particular ways. It also corners people, severely limiting their choices so that their behavior appears almost predetermined. No matter what the actions of people are in Thull, Islam always affects their consequences. Finally, Islam creates and releases powerful emotions, which propel people toward certain behaviors despite personal costs by virtue of the part these play in constructing self.

CULTURE, SELF, AND EMOTIONS

Three interconnected ideas help explain the relation between Islam and *dushmani*: culture, self, and emotions. The literature informing these ideas is too extensive to discuss here. I recommend as a place to start, "Grief and the Headhunter's Rage" by Renato Rosaldo (1984); *The Social Construction of Emotions,* edited by Rom Harré (1986); and *Unnatural Emotions* by Katherine A. Lutz (1988) for those wishing to explore these ideas further.

Anthropologists think about culture in a variety of ways; it would waste time to argue the strengths and weaknesses of various definitions here. For the purposes of this book, culture is simply the system of meaning in terms of which people interact. The concept of self is more slippery. The "'me'ness of me" or, alternatively, "the uniqueness of the individual" captures its fundamental meaning. One's sense of forming a *unified* being with some continuing control over life and circumstances provides a good way of thinking about it, according to Carl Sagan. Patients lose self when doctors perform prefrontal lobotomies, as he tells us in *The Dragons of Eden* (1977:103). Hence self apparently possesses some physiological basis common to the human condition.

Although self may be universal to *Homo sapiens,* people create specific selves from shared systems of meaning, that is to say, cultures. Moreover individuals construct self primarily from the repertoire of identities they find around them. By identities I do not mean only statuses like parent/child, husband/wife, leader/follower, which are linked together in pairs by formal rights and obligations. The notion of identity is more inclusive, encompassing, along with formal statuses—the nurturing mother, the bad dude, the intellectual, the valley girl, the pious Muslim, for example. We can think of identities as idealized templates defined by shared values drawn from wider systems of meaning. Such templates provide goals people strive toward in becoming who they are.

While identities do not always connect to one another as paired opposites, they do interrelate, though legalistic rights and obligations do not necessarily unite them. On the contrary, identities associate in ways similar to the relationships one finds among overlapping color transparencies. People construct self from overlapping transparency-like identities whose various pigments taken together color them in a changing variety of hues. Consequently, we can think of self as a system, patterned by the interrelationships among its various identities.

This brings us to the relationship between self and emotions, and particularly to the effect this relationship has on *dushmani.* Understanding death enmity in Thull requires understanding the role of emotions in maintaining the integrity of self. The importance of emotions in organized vengeance is powerfully expressed in *Land Without Justice* (1958), Milovan Djilas' autobiography of his childhood in Montenegro. During the early 20th century, when Djilas was a boy, blood feuding pervaded the lives of the Montenegrin people. Not surprisingly, revenge loomed large in their thoughts. As he tells us:

> Revenge is an overpowering and consuming fire. It flares up and burns away every other thought and emotion. Only it remains, over and above everything else. . . . Vengeance—this is a breath of life one shares from the cradle with one's fellow clansmen, in both good fortune and bad, vengeance from eternity. . . . It was our clan, and Uncle Mirko—his love and suffering and the years of unfulfilled desire for revenge and for life. Vengeance is not hatred, but the wildest and sweetest kind of drunkenness, both for those who must wreak vengeance and for those who wish to be avenged. (1958:106–107)

Djilas' text suggests that one can understand organized violence in Montenegro by relating it to emotions made up of feelings and actions twisted around one another. Specifically he shows how feeling revenge, while at the same time striving to accomplish it, helps Montenegrins preserve self. Such emotions are cultural constructs, defined by shared systems of meaning, and called forth by culturally specific kinds of events. Emotional responses, therefore, inextricably connect to self, primarily as passions. If expressing and feeling certain emotions in appropriate situations defines cultural identities critical to self, then people either respond with these emotions or find self disintegrating. Consequently they will experience such emotions as something that happens to them over which they possess little control, in other words, as passions. The social psychologist James Averill explains the relationship between passions and self in more detail in *Anger and Aggression: An Essay on Emotion* (1982). The approach outlined here owes much to his thinking.

The authors of many blood feud accounts often describe the act of taking vengeance as distinct from the feelings of hatred and anger that motivate it. Thinking about emotions as we have here forces us to look at vengeance in new ways. Because Americans construct the emotions we call anger and hatred, one cannot assume they universally exist. The emotion relevant to blood feuds in Montenegro, for instance, appears to be neither anger nor hatred, but vengeance itself. Moreover, feeling vengeance as a kind of wild sweet drunkenness differs from the way most Americans feel either anger or hatred, which shows that vengeance emotions in Montenegro are as much culturally constructed by Montenegrins as they are biologically natural to *homo Sapiens*. Our approach also blurs the difference between vengeance as inner feeling and outer response, seeing both to be equally a part of the emotional experience. Finally, understanding the relation between emotions and self helps us understand the compelling force of vengeance. It can so forcefully define identities critical to self that one experiences it as a passion, compelling one to feel and act in particular ways.

Writing about emotions, self, and culture in concrete terms as done above, conceals a trap. It urges us to cast them in stone, to think of them as things and, therefore, relatively unchanging. But we must always remember their processual quality. They "happen" in a variety of situations: at cocktail parties, on the beach, during ritual performances, on pickup basketball courts, during college classes. They occur as verbs as well as nouns, in the active as well as passive voice.

Events—a ritual performance, an anthropology class meeting, a beach party—do not just reflect culture, emotions, and self. People also create and recreate them as they participate in the events; as the events flow one into another, participants fashion ever-shifting versions of them. Nonetheless what people create can turn on them, channeling their behavior and propelling them toward particular courses of action. Such an approach lends itself especially well to blood feuding in Thull, for it helps explain what powers *dushmani*. In the pages that follow we will see how Muslim identity organizes self, how Muslim identity incorporates revenge, and, thus, how the passion for revenge becomes a compelling force.

THE AXIOMATIC FEATURES OF ISLAM

Islam possesses a simple beauty and exquisite complexity at the same time. I can only describe a small part of Islam here, for volumes fail to treat its subtleties and intricacies in their entirety. I can, however, outline some of the more significant characteristics for the people of Thull, especially those related to *dushmani*. I once asked a Kohistani friend to tell me the most important aspects of Islam. He answered, "the *Kalima,* prayer, fast, and faith." These four features make up the heart of Islam in Thull, although others are also meaningful to Kohistanis. And basic to their belief is a conception of God.

God in Thull does not resemble some distant father who rarely sees his children except during Christmas and Easter, or on Sunday morning. No. God in Thull "sticks right in your face." Constantly repeating "Allah" in formal greetings, casual conversations, and even in most arguments makes God's presence a part of everyday reality. His relevancy is overwhelmingly clear to everyone. Additionally Allah does not wear the clothes of a loving parent but appears as an imperious ruler, who demands that his subjects unconditionally submit to his will. Fundamentally Islam means submission (as well as peace, with the implication that one achieves peace by submitting to God's will).

Submitting to God's will is the first fundamental component of Islamic faith, bearing witness to its central truths the second. One generally bears witness by reciting the lines of the *Kalima.*

> I witness that Allah is the only God.
> I witness that Allah is the only God.
> I witness that Mohammed is his prophet.
> I witness that Mohammed is his prophet.

Reciting the *Kalima* automatically makes one a Muslim, according to the people of Thull. Consequently, when I attempted to elicit Kohistani vocabulary from village children, they often tried to trick me into converting to Islam by telling me the Arabic words of the *Kalima* instead. Pious Kohistanis keep the *Kalima* close to their lips, for they must continually witness their faith by reciting its words. The constant repetition helps create and recreate Muslim identity, and situates Islam at the center of self.

The *Kalima* forms a pivotal part of Muslim prayer, and praying constitutes the most notable act of submission to God the people of Thull perform. Religious leaders constantly exhort Kohistanis to pray. Mullana Fakir, leader of the largest mosque in Thull, even preaches that men should admonish their wives to pray. "If they don't," he advises, "then beat them. If they still don't, then divorce them."

THE RITUAL OF PRAYER

While reading the following account of Muslim prayer, one might question the need for such detailed ethnographic description. But prayer brings into play dominant symbols and arouses powerful emotions that continually fashion and refashion an organization of self circling Muslim identity. This process is revealed in the complexity of Muslim prayer. Moreover, experiencing firsthand the complexity of detail will help the reader understand the critical importance of prayer to Kohistanis, although in themselves the details may appear inconsequential.

The language of Muslim prayer is Arabic. Hence Kohistanis intone their prayers in a ritual language that many understand either incompletely, or not at all. Consequently praying is a time-consuming and demanding task, as the complexity of the following description (which repeats the Kohistani pronunciation of Arabic words) makes evident. Yet Kohistanis believe that saying one's prayers correctly and at the specified times is the minimal obligation of good Muslims. Few fail to fulfill this obligation.

Prayer in Thull is of two kinds, *du'a* and *namaz*. Kohistanis say *du'a* prayers in a variety of contexts. For example, after eating they give thanks to God in a kind of prayer called *du'ai shukraraj*. When someone dies, people pray that his/her soul may rest in peace, intoning a *du'ai maghfarat,* and those initiating any kind of major project (constructing a house, for instance) say a *du'ai barkat.* Purifying the worshipper by raising the hands to touch facial orifices marks *du'a* prayers.

The pious always say *du'a* prayers on all appropriate occasions, but when most Kohistanis talk about saying their prayers, they mean *namaz. Namaz* forms a ritual cycle that punctuates each day at five specified times. While all *namaz* rituals vary on a common theme, each has its own peculiarities and each its own name:

Fajar—the morning prayer said just before dawn
Zohar—the noon prayer
Asar—the afternoon prayer said about 5:30 P.M.
Maghrib—the evening prayer said just after sunset
Isha—the night prayer said about 9:30 P.M.

The call to prayer, called *azan,* always initiates *namaz.* Usually, a religious leader—a *mullana, mulvi,* or *mullah*—chants *azan* from the mosque, which signals all those in the nearby vicinity to gather for prayer. Sometimes the leader of the mosque asks a guest to give *azan,* especially if he possesses skill at chanting. In the hands of a skilled chanter, *azan* has a beauty and power to evoke emotions difficult to describe adequately. *Azan* translates as follows:

God is great!
God is great!
I witness that no one is worthy of worship except God.
I witness that no one is worthy of worship except God.
I witness that Mohammed is the prophet of God.
I witness that Mohammed is the prophet of God.
Come to prayer.
Come to prayer.
Come to success.
Come to success.
God is great.
God is great.
No one is worthy of worship except God.

The call to *Fajar,* the morning prayer, varies slightly in that the chanter inserts the twice repeated phrase "Prayer is better than sleep," immediately following the second "Come to success." At 5:30 in the morning this always made me think the Prophet (peace be upon him) possessed a definite sense of humor.

As the men gather (Islam forbids women to enter mosques; they must pray alone), each faces the holy city of Mecca in Saudi Arabia to perform a sequence of prescribed rituals by himself. When the majority finish, the worshippers, called *muktadids,* form rows headed by an *imam* ("leader"), again all facing toward Mecca. A ritual specialist appointed by the *imam,* called a *moazan,* begins by intoning the *aqamat.* This comprises a special version of *azan,* distinguished by the twice-repeated phrase "Stand still for prayer," inserted after "Come to success." The *imam* then chants "God is great," and the main part of the ritual begins.

Complex units of ritual action, called *rakats,* make up *namaz.* (See figure 2.) Like *namaz* itself, *rakats* vary—in small but significant details of ritual action and in function. Distinctive dimensions of contrast differentiate four kinds of *rakats: faras, sunnat, nafal,* and *vitar.* Worshippers render the ritual actions of *faras rakats* collectively under the leadership of the *imam,* who chants its phrases while performing the other three *rakats* individually, their phrases repeated silently. Kohistanis must perform both *sunnat* and *vitar rakats* (failing to do so constitutes a serious sin). They distinguish between them by their contrastive purposes. Worshippers render *sunnat rakats* for the holy prophet, *vitar rakats* for themselves. Conversely, people can choose not to perform *nafal rakats,* though doing so demonstrates piety and helps the worshipper gain paradise.

Both number, sequence, and kind of *rakats* change with various kinds of *namaz* prayer. *Fajar* has two *sunnat rakats,* for example, whereas *zohar* has six. *Maghrib* has three *faras rakats* whereas *isha* has four. And only *isha* has *vitar rakats,* three in all. Sequences of body movements in conjunction with spoken phrases constitute the *rakats* themselves. Raising the hands to the ears, crossing the arms over the stomach, bowing while placing the hands

	Sunnat	Faras	Sunnat	Nafal	Vitar	Nafal
Fajar	2	2	/////	/////	/////	/////
Zohar	4	4	2	2	/////	/////
Asar	4	4	/////	/////	/////	/////
Maghrib	/////	3	2	2	/////	/////
Isha	4	4	2	2	3	3

Figure 2   Rakats of Muslim Prayer

on the knees, prostrating the body with the head touching the ground, and raising the index finger while moving it from one ear to the other comprise some of the movements. Lines from the Koran and the *Kalima,* affirmations of God's greatness, and formulaic blessings and praises to God make up the core of the spoken phrases. The phrases and movements intertwine in involved and complex progressions.

A careful look at the verbal and kinetic components of *namaz* points out that prayer in Thull does not so much communicatively link Man with God. On the contrary, it asserts fundamental truths of Islam. Pointing the index finger asserts God's oneness. Crossing the arms over the stomach, bowing while placing the hands on the knees, and touching the head to the ground submit the worshipper to God, the imperious ruler. Similarly, such verbal phrases as "God is great!," "Praises are for my God who is great!," "All good traits are for God!," and "All praises are for my God who is best!" profess the greatness of God in relation to the humbleness of humans.

In sum, *namaz* prayer in Thull involves long and complex rituals. It demands that participants devote considerable time and concentration to worship. By doing so, *namaz* dedicates and rededicates worshippers to Islam, and in the process recreates Muslim identities located at the center of self.

THE RITUAL OF FAST

Keeping the fast during *Ramazan* (called *Ramadan* in the western part of the Muslim world), the month-long period set aside for that purpose, distinguishes pious Muslims from those who casually follow Islam's precepts. Repeated exhortations to fast and to pray make up two of the triumvirate themes dominating religious preaching in Thull. No one in the community publicly admits to breaking the fast. Accordingly, accusing anyone in Thull of failing to fast constitutes a serious charge that can lead to fighting, bloodshed, and even murder.

Fasting has simple, unambiguous rules; during Ramazan nothing should pass one's lips during the time between the calls to morning and evening prayers. Particularly Muslims should not eat, drink, smoke, or take snuff. Nor should Muslims reorganize their daily activities to escape feeling the uncomfortable effects of the fast. One should not sleep excessive amounts of time during the day but, to the contrary, should fully experience fasting so that one contemplates and, most importantly, wholly embraces Islamic faith. Keeping the fast, therefore, continually reinvigorates the power of Muslim identity to dominate self.

The Islamic faith (*iman*) that must be wholly embraced includes belief in angels; in God's omnipotence and His oneness; in a day of judgment; and in the sending by God of a series of prophets to spread the divine message on earth, Mohammad being the last of the series. Muslims believe God will send no one to follow Mohammad because he brought mankind the perfect truth. *Iman* has an additional meaning to Kohistanis as well. They also understand it as a particular kind of gift from God consisting primarily of *ghrairat* (honor in the sense of personal integrity). God gives *ghrairat* to all male Muslims at birth. No Kohistani can gain it by his actions, but anyone can lose *ghrairat* by failing to protect it. With few exceptions, protecting *ghrairat* requires taking revenge. Kohistanis believe Muslims must protect God's gift by taking vengeance at appropriate times, or they forsake their obligations to him. Kohistani notions of *iman* thus inject vengeance into Muslim identity and help create sociocultural contexts that incubate death enmity.

The pace of life in Thull dramatically changes during *Ramazan.* A kind of tense stillness hovers in the air. Both speech and the way men move their bodies, become slow, studied, controlled, and a faint threat of violence continually lurks just beneath the surface. Hunger and thirst create volatile tempers, and embracing *iman* means embracing one's obligations for vengeance. *Ramazan* is the season for revenge, as everyone in Thull knows.

FUNDAMENTALIST ISLAM IN THULL

Religious beliefs in Thull form an especially streamlined version of Sunni Islam. The *Kalima,* prayer, fast, giving alms to the poor and making the pilgrimage to Mecca compose what Muslims everywhere call "the five pillars of Islam." Kohistanis recognize that one should contribute alms and give considerable respect to those who make the pilgrimage. They show much less concern for these last two obligations, however, because the *Kalima,* prayer, and fast constitute more fundamental "pillars."

Yet Sunni fundamentalism in Kohistan differs from the brand of Shi'a Islam so politically significant in Iran and Lebanon. Religious figures in Thull do not boast the kind of institutionalized political authority possessed by fundamentalist Shi'a leaders. I will talk more about the power of religion in Kohistani politics (a power made even more effective by its subtlety) in a later chapter. Here I need only note that Kohistanis differentiate among religious leaders by their knowledge of Islam.

Still, the men occupying positions ranked by degrees of religious competency have no secular authority. In other words, the titles they hold do not confer special rights to make secular political decisions binding on members of the community. People think of them primarily as scholars, men whose special learning gives them the right to speak with authority only on matters pertaining to religion. Mullana Fakir, for instance, never gave his opinions in council debates, nor would anyone have listened to him if he had. Nevertheless he spoke unhesitatingly to the throng that gathered around two accident victims at a wedding. A man had attempted to ignite a dynamite stick during the celebration, but the fuse had burned too fast, exploding the dynamite prematurely. The explosion blew off the man's hand and blinded a young bystander. When the crowd heard Mullana Fakir's voice coming over the loud-speaker in the mosque, conversation immediately hushed. He spoke authoritatively and directly to the point. "Exploding dynamite at weddings is un-Islamic, like singing and dancing, and should cease!" People listened with respect.

Islam in Thull also differs from more orthodox fundamentalism found in other parts of the Muslim world by a special set of accretions. These elements of Islamic ideology focus on death enmity, molding it in specific ways. Kohistanis have competed with their politically powerful Pathan neighbors for centuries. Accordingly the peculiar nature of Pathan Islam made a deep and lasting impact on Kohistani culture. Pathans differentiate themselves from surrounding people by strictly adhering to a tribal code of conduct called *pakhtunwali*. At its core lie four obligations: to commit vengeance, to provide hospitality, to give refuge to anyone asking for it (even a mortal enemy), and to treat with generosity a fallen advisory who sues for peace. *Pakhtunwali* and Islam interconnect in Pathan culture in an ambiguous way. Most Pathans claim their common ancestor converted to Islam at an early date, allegedly becoming one of the first of Mohammad's converts. Consequently most Pathans see themselves as archetypal Muslims, believing their way of life to be fundamentally and profoundly Islamic. At the same time, Pathans set themselves above other Muslims by strictly adhering to their distinctive code of conduct. Some Pathans will occasionally admit that *pakhtunwali* superficially makes them poor Muslims, because orthodox Islamic teaching does not recognize it. Nonetheless they declare everything Pathan to be Islamic, almost by definition. I heard an educated Pathan, a graduate student in a major American university, argue for the Islamic quality of Pathan culture. He said in the same breath, "No. Of course *pakhtunwali* is not Islamic. But yes, it is Islamic."

Kohistanis borrowed the essential features of *pakhtunwali* over the last three hundred years of contact with the Yusufzai, the dominant Pathan group in Dir. Taking revenge, providing hospitality, giving refuge, and being generous to a fallen enemy became accepted rules of behavior in Thull. Even so, no Kohistani ever claimed to follow *pakhtunwali,* for one must be Pathan to do that. Nevertheless Kohistanis accepted the rules of *pakhtunwali* as integral to Islam because they bought Pathans' claims to be archetypal Muslims. Friends unhesitatingly told me that because the Koran (the holy book of God) and the Hadith (the holy prophet's sayings) prominently displayed them, following these rules demonstrated Muslim piety. Revenge, consequently, became a defining characteristic of the Muslim identity located at the center of self.

THE BROTHERHOOD OF PREACHERS

To better understand how Islam in Thull empowers revenge we must also discuss the most recent change in Kohistani religion, the birth of the *Tablighi Jamma'at* or *Jamma'at al-Tabligh.* In the last few years this organization surged through Pakistan, as well as Pakistani communities in the United States and Europe, like a hurricane tidal wave. *Tablighi Jamma'at* ("community of evangelists," or "preachers") even operates in Muslim areas of the Soviet Union according to members in Thull. Unquestionably the organization has become one of the most potent forces in Kohistan.

The Community of Preachers dedicates itself to uniting Muslims of all sects and persuasions so that Islam can counteract the power of secular Western states. The organization argues that all Muslims must unite to struggle effectively against the powers of Satan. Accordingly it emphasizes those aspects of Islam unifying Muslims (the five pillars of Islam and correct moral behavior), while minimizing the sectarian, ethnic, regional, and national differences dividing them.

Tablighi Jamma'at began sometime in the 1950s in the village of Raivind near Lahore in the Punjab. Mullana Mohammed Zikria, a wealthy textile mill owner and noted religious scholar, founded the organization. His book *Tablighi Nisab*, "Syllabus for Preaching," remains today the group's charter of purpose, and copies exist in most rural villages in Pakistan. Muslim scholars translated the book into several South Asian languages; a Pushto version resides in the library of the main mosque in Thull. Raivind remains today the center for the group's activities, it's headquarters located in a large mosque and *madrasa* (religious school) in that village. The community of scholars in residence there forms a kind of semiofficial leadership for the organization. Once each year members from all over the world gather in Raivind, while similar, but smaller, gatherings periodically occur in the various administrative districts in Pakistan. Chitral hosted a gathering numbering more than 1000 members in 1984.

No clear-cut rules dictate *Tablighi* membership, for any man can join. Participating in the group's preaching automatically makes one a member, and those who take part regularly become known as *tablighis*, or "preachers." Members of the group begin their activities by visiting the people living in a chosen locality, usually near members' homes. At other times *tablighis* travel to different neighborhoods in the same community. Sometimes deputations journey outside their home villages, and on rare occasions even outside their native country. Men in Thull visited cities in India, and one man from London visited Thull as a member of a *Tablighi* deputation. When traveling in distant areas the group sleeps at a local mosque, visiting the homes of the people who frequent it.

Those wishing to participate in the activities of the group in Thull gather at a chosen mosque about one hour before noon or afternoon prayer. After the members assemble they choose a leader (*amir*), who in turn appoints a spokesman (*mutakalam*). The group then leaves the mosque to begin their duties, headed by the leader. *Tablighi* deputations walk in single file, with heads bowed, and with a look of sanctity on their faces. The members carry bedding on their heads when they plan to spend the night at the mosque. There they propound Islamic morality to one another and anyone else who happens to be present.

Members of the deputation recite the *Kalima*, the affirmation of faith, repeatedly to themselves, as they walk with their heads bowed. No one speaks aloud except the spokesman. He talks only when the group encounters a man on the path or at the door of his house. He says, "We are from the mosque. Because of God's blessings we are Muslims. Our deeds should be as our words. Please join us in our virtuous work." Most men cannot refuse the invitation. About fifteen minutes before the call to prayer, the deputation, swollen in size by those who joined along the way, turns toward the mosque. After it arrives, the spokesman asks everyone present to remain after prayer for preaching to be led by the *amir,* although other members of the group participate if they wish. Preaching focuses on prayer, fast, and moral behavior. "Moral behavior" signifies the morality of Muslims as contrasted to the evil decadence of Kafirs, for *Tablighi* preaching continually propounds the holiness of Islam relative to the sinfulness of Kafirs. Participation in the group's activities creates new contexts for constructing Muslim identity and reinforces a self defined primarily in its terms. Emphasizing moral behavior also reinforces the passion for revenge, as discussed below.

WOMEN, HONOR, AND REVENGE

Moral behavior leads us to the third major theme in sermons (whether sermons of recognized religious scholars, or preachings of the *Tablighi Jamma'at*), and the last feature of Islam to be considered here. Along with saying prayers and keeping the fast, preachers in Thull repeatedly admonish men to control their women. Women's behavior becomes a matter of male Muslim identity because the way women act directly impacts on *ghrairat,* men's gift of personal integrity from God. Women must never walk outside their husband's (or father's) house without proper escort, preachers proclaim. Women must never speak to an unrelated man. No man's direct gaze should fall on another's wife or daughter. Women (men too, but especially women) must not sing or dance, particularly at weddings. Finally, women should always comport themselves with modesty to protect their shame (*sharam*)—hiding, controlling, minimizing, and denying their sexuality completely if possible. Men who allow their women freedom become *baghrairatman* ("men without personal integrity"). So do those who refuse to retaliate violently against anyone purposely threatening their women's shame.

The number of women whose shame puts a man's integrity at risk varies with the situation, but can be extensive. This factor alone intensifies death enmity in the community. Wives, daughters, and sisters always possess the power to endanger men's integrity. Additionally, men's vulnerability can extend to other women under a variety of circumstances. The men who owned the house where I lived always guarded my research assistant's wife with their rifles whenever she left our compound. Yet they knew she needed little protection, as only a minimal threat to her physical safety existed. But because she lived in their house, any attack on her shame by men outside the household, even a simple stare, threatened their integrity as well. By guarding her, they guarded themselves.

Men's vulnerability to attacks on women's shame can even stretch further than the household. Once I asked Anwar to arrange a visit to a Kohistani house in the neighboring Swat Valley for a group of American teachers traveling through Pakistan under the auspices of the Fullbright program. After we finished our obligatory tea and left the house, a woman in the group asked one of the Kohistani men present to have his picture taken with her. Unfortunately, Kohistanis interpret such actions as explicit sexual invitations; the man responded by attempting to embrace her. Visibly shaken, she asked me to tell Anwar, but I refused, knowing the potential for deadly violence in the situation. "Terrific!" I thought, as I imagined the field day newspapers and magazines would have with the story if anyone were killed.

I did tell Anwar what occurred three days later, after we returned to Thull. He immediately demanded to know the name of the culprit. He arranged the visit, making him responsible for the women in the group, and putting his personal integrity at risk. "Why didn't you tell me this immediately? I should have given the man an instant gift of bullets! Tell me who he is now, so I can kill him! He has made my *ghrairat* (personal integrity) bad." Fortunately, I did not know the man's name.

Our study of Islam in Thull concentrated on the relation between religious ideology and death enmity. We learned how men create and recreate vengeance as part of a Muslim identity crucial in constructing self, and how vengeance becomes a passion, endowed with the power to move men to violence. Yet the religious ideology I have described is unorthodox in many ways. Understanding how it became such an important part of Kohistani culture will help to explain what generated blood feuding in Thull. Accordingly, I take a historical perspective in the next chapter, tracing the sociocultural transformations leading to changes in religious ideology. At the same time, changes in Thull's economic system also worked to implement death enmity, reinforcing the effects of changes in the system of Islamic beliefs.

4 / The Genesis
of *Dushmani*

Death enmity became the centerpiece of Thull social organization only in the last few decades. How can we account for its appearance such a short time ago? Part of the answer lies in the relation between Islamic ideology, Muslim identity, and self that gives *dushmani* the power to influence behavior, as we saw in the last chapter. But we still need to know how this relationship developed through time. In other words we must take a historical perspective, one that considers *dushmani* in terms of sociocultural change.

I should emphasize that such a perspective does not abandon the notion of system. Organized vengeance may be an integral part of a system, but it is one that has depth in time. Its systematic qualities are most analogous to a weather system—structurally ordered to be sure, but dynamic as well: a system ever in flux, whose interrelated parts are as much processes as forms (Hallpike 1977:275–277). Death enmity in Thull resembles the eye of a hurricane: It lies at the center of a system; it stands in dynamic relationship with entities enfolding it; and it formed historically as the result of complex processes. *Dushmani,* in other words, must be understood as a procedure in time—its contemporary structure seen as resulting from a long history of sociocultural transformations. The story begins with the organization of Kohistani society in the pre-Islamic period, 400 years ago.

PRE-ISLAMIC SOCIAL ORGANIZATION

Based on what is known of contemporary pagan tribes in the area, social organization during the pre-Islamic period probably centered on the exchange of women among exogamous lineages. Women did not seclude themselves; relationships between men and women were relatively free and open; and the sexual purity of women did not predicate notions of honor. This is not to say that disputes over women were not politically volatile. Wife stealing was a major source of internal political conflict, as accounts of contemporary pagan tribes show. Nevertheless wife stealing, although an attack on a husband's rights, did not involve honor. Consequently men could peacefully settle such cases by paying fines and compensation more often than not. Moreover wife stealing struck at important political alliances between lineages built on ties of marriage. Paternal relatives of both opponents in such disputes generally applied pressure for their peaceful settlement in order to maintain these alliances.

Leadership institutions and political values in pagan times probably reflected the general insecurity in the region. Communities drew their leaders from lineage elders chosen *ad hoc* for the specific problem at hand. One of their most important duties was maintaining village peace through the nonviolent resolution of internal disputes. Factionalism would dangerously weaken the community's ability to deal effectively with external threats without such efforts.

Village peace as a political value was an important force in many pagan societies in the eastern Hindu-Kush. Among the Kom tribe in Afghanistan near the Pakistan border, for example, people so valued village harmony that elders forced disputants to settle their differences peacefully. The Kom recognized that uncontrolled violence posed a serious threat to their continued existence. Hence community leaders expelled murderers and confiscated their property (Robertson 1896:439–442). No rules precluded taking immediate vengeance, but those who chose to accept compensation instead of revenge received high praise from their fellows. Similar customs reported by Barth for Swat Kohistan make it probable that Kohistani communities treated murder and revenge in a similar manner during the pre-Islamic period in Dir. Even today in Thull, *lamo aman* ("village peace") is a respected value, and to be called *aman pasand* ("peace lover") an honored compliment. Lineage elders still negotiate dispute settlements, although their efforts in murder cases often fail.

The members of pagan tribes did recognize the legitimacy of some retaliatory vengeance murders. Among the Kom, men committed retaliatory vengeance killings, but they directed vengeance outside the community to members of surrounding tribes. For example, men raided Pathan villages in retaliation for their alleged killing of a Kom culture hero (Richard Strand, personal communication). Today *dushmani* sometimes exists between Kohistani communities as well as between individuals. The villages of Kalkot and Birikot have a relationship of enmity going back fifteen years. Because of it, fifteen men lost their lives.

In all probability, then, organized vengeance did form a part of the social order in pre-Islamic Kohistan—though not related to honor based on sexual purity of women, and limited to intercommunity relations. Intracommunity peace was critical for survival in an environment where force often decided political differences between settlements. Networks of alliance and hostility among communities cast in terms of organized vengeance provided a degree of order in an otherwise anarchical situation. Indeed *dushmani* in Thull goes far back in time.

CONVERSION TO ISLAM

The cultural values, concepts, and ideas so important to organized vengeance in contemporary Thull were probably introduced at the same time Pathan missionaries converted the Kohistanis to Islam. Their effect on existing social organization and culture set in motion processes of change that ultimately resulted in a new, unique Kohistani sociocultural system—a system, however, neither logically consistent, nor tightly structured. On the contrary, a changing field of tensions and contradictions exerted forces of varying strength on different individuals at different times.

It appears likely that immediately after conversion to Islam the core of Kohistani social organization and culture remained generally unchanged. Barth reports that as late as 1954 seclusion did not organize women's lives and that both men and women enjoyed free and open relationships in Kohistani villages in the Swat valley (1956:66). Similarly informants in Thull stated that the rules of strict *purdah* now in force are recent, occurring only in the last few decades. Barth's male informants stated no preference for marrying any category of women and, in particular, no preference for marriage with close paternal cousins (1956:66). This differs considerably from the claims of strict paternal cousin marriage one hears today, although it unquestionably represents a change from the strict lineage exogamy of the pagan period.

Politics within Kohistani communities probably remained unchanged as well. Barth's information on Kohistani politics, as we have seen, shows a system similar in form to contemporary pagan tribes in the area. In the unstable conditions that continued after the Kohistanis converted to Islam, the political unity of communities remained crucial for their survival. Organized vengeance within communities probably remained, as a result, too threatening to be permitted. Nevertheless, the forces of sociocultural change set in motion by contact with Pathan culture and conversion to Islam had increasing impact on patterns of organized vengeance in Kohistan, as events in the outside world continued to modify the political milieu in which the Kohistani communities existed.

THULL UNDER THE *NAWABS*

A Pathan chief in southern Dir finally conquered Dir Kohistan in 1888, and his successors, known as *nawabs*, succeeded in subjecting Thull and its neighbors to the vagaries of their rule—largely because of British imperial policy during the years of the Raj. Throughout the days of the British Raj, maintaining a friendly government in Dir strong enough to protect the road to Chitral formed a cornerstone of British colonial policy on the Northwest Frontier. As long as the *nawabs* protected the road and allowed the British Army to use it, the Raj was satisfied. The government provided them arms, subsidies, specially arranged meetings with the Viceroy in Simla, and *carte blanche* to rule as they saw fit.

The rulers of Dir built their political policy upon twin pillars: loyalty to the British Raj and a tenacious adherence to traditional Pathan values. Unlike the rulers of neighboring Swat, who pursued a policy of social and economic development, the *nawabs* strove to maintain Dir as a patrimonial state. They neither adopted nor developed any kind of formal legal code to regularize their rule, instead governing by arbitrary decrees determined only by whimsy. Moreover they constructed few roads. The highway linking Dir to Chitral was the only notable exception, but the British insisted they build that road. Consequently most communities remained physically isolated and at least partially quarantined from political, ideological, and economic developments outside Dir. Finally, in order to weaken potential opposition, the *nawabs* actively encouraged local strife. At the same time, they suppressed armed conflicts between the communities of Dir and Chitral at the demand of their British patrons.

The *nawabs'* policies effected particular cultural changes in Thull. To promote contention within communities they encouraged blood vengeance by levying light fines for murder, at the same time advocating that injured parties retaliate rather than accept compensation. They instituted this policy under the guise of promoting *badal* ("revenge"), a key value in *pakhtunwali,* the code of the Pathans.

Nevertheless institutionalized vengeance did not become an important element in social relations, though Kohistanis came to recognize *badal* as an important value. A look at the relationship among Kohistani values, politics, economics and social organization during the *nawabs'* reign will elucidate why this was so.

The Pathan value of *badal* ("revenge") contradicted *aman pasand,* the indigenous Kohistani value of "village peace," which exerted counteracting force. It also contradicted the way prestige and leadership operated. Leadership in Thull depended on possessing *aizzat* ("prestige"), which, among other things, depended on having good relationships with other men in the community. Peacefully settling one's disputes helped maintain good relations. But *badal* required violent retaliation. If a man continually refused to settle disputes peacefully, then too often troubled relations resulted, lessening his prestige and weakening his ability to achieve leadership. Moreover, members of patrilineages chose leaders to represent their interests, and they suspected a man generally unwilling to forego personal revenge, for he might overly concern himself with furthering his own ends. Hence countervailing forces compelling men to make peace tempered the power of *badal.* Though vengeance became an accepted value in Kohistani culture, it was only one of many often contradictory forces, which partially explains why it did not result in widespread *dushmani.*

The configuration of moral values was not the only force inhibiting the development of *dushmani* during the *nawabs'* reign. Intercommunity political relationships, ecology, social organization, and the *nawabs'* refusal to build roads were also relevant factors. During the *nawabs'* rule a balance between alpine herding and agriculture formed the basis for subsistence in Kohistan. In the winter herd owners kept goats and cattle in special quarters in or near permanent settlements, whereas in the summer they took their animals into the mountains to graze on the rich grass found in high alpine meadows. Men generally did the herding; women cultivated maize in the fields surrounding the permanent settlements. Beyond the subsistence herding and cultivation provided, both also provided cash income. Men transported by foot the cheese and ghee produced in the mountains to surrounding market centers for sale.

Herding was a chancy operation at best. Disease, accidents, and sudden changes in weather common in the high mountains struck at random, often decimating herds. Kohistanis raided herds in Chitral to recoup animal losses in earlier years. After the *nawab*s incorporated Thull into Dir State, however, raiding Chitral became uneconomical because they harshly punished raiders at the insistence of the British. Consequently conflicts within the community significantly increased. Disputes over stray animals and arguments about animal theft became common, and strife turned inward.

Yet *dushmani* did not develop as one might expect, although playing off opponents exacerbated disputes within communities. The reason lies partly in the nature of descent group organization and the rules distributing rights to pasture. The people of Thull divide into three patrilineal clans, each in turn splitting into various lineages. Clans used to have important ceremonial functions (no longer operant) and often opposed one another in political contexts during the era of the *nawab*s. When disputes erupted between lineages of different clans, other lineages often became involved through ties of common clanship. Hence the potential existed for disputes between lineages to grow until large numbers of people became involved. Indeed physical fights broke out on occasion, involving most males in the community.

Rules allocating pastures, however, reduced the acrimony of conflicts. Summer pastures in Thull divide into distinct units, each with a particular name and well-defined boundaries. Thull allocates these pasture units to herding groups for a one-year period. Lineages from all three clans compose each herding group. Thus people who herded together, who had common rights to pastures and common interest in protecting these rights, were often those who opposed one another in clan disputes.

This was a classic system of cross-cutting allegiances. Men joined with others as members of clans and, as such, shared political interests and moral sentiments. But they joined with others as members of herding groups. Interests and sentiments cross-cut one another, then, and resolving conflicts in loyalties through settling disputes dovetailed with the value of maintaining village peace. Despite the increase in intracommunity contention, dispute settlement mechanisms successfully operated to settle conflict, for both moral values and political-economic interests existed for doing so.

The *nawab*s' failure to build an extensive road system had two consequences for inhibiting the growth of *dushmani*. First, it physically isolated the Kohistani communities. Thull and her neighbors inhabit a high mountain valley, which connected to the rest of Dir by narrow treacherous footpaths during the time of the *nawab*s. People found communicating with distant settlements difficult in the best of weather, and impossible when snow and mud slides blocked the mountain tracks. The *nawab*s' representatives could not visit Kohistan much of the time, as a result, which left power in the institutions of the indigenous political system. Public assemblies continued to make political decisions, and lineage leaders continued to mediate disputes in terms of local custom and morality. Thus her institutions for dispute settlement remained largely intact, even though Thull existed as a part of Dir State.

Even more important, the lack of roads limited economic development, which in turn limited the amount of cash individuals could accumulate so few Kohistanis could purchase rifles. During the era of the *nawab*s the most common weapons in Kohistan were clubs, knives, stabbing spears, and slings. Men found it difficult to kill with these weapons because their effective use demanded proximity to the intended victim, at best a difficult task to accomplish. Consequently, disputes that escalated to violence did not usually result in murder. Opponents could peacefully settle such disputes more easily than murder cases because they did not arouse as violent emotions. Even in murder cases, men were often (though not always) willing to accept compensation because they found retaliatory killing so difficult to successfully carry out.

Internal conflict and tension came to permeate Thull politics during this time. Still, because of social institutions, cultural values, and particular features of the larger system of which Thull was a part, institutionalized vengeance did not pervade social relationships. The value of *badal* became an accepted part of Kohistani culture, at the same time, and intracommunity strife an expected part of personal relations.

INDEPENDENCE

Pakistani officials assumed admistrative duties in the Northwest Frontier Province following independence in 1947, although the Nawab maintained control over internal affairs in Dir. When tension developed between the Nawab and Pakistani officials over his opposition to social and economic development, the government forcibly deposed him, and in 1965 assumed direct administration of Dir. A new era began, one marked by far-reaching change.

The Pakistani Government immediately embarked on an ambitious program of social and economic development. Government agencies built a large, modern hospital complex in Timargara, Dir's administrative center. They constructed schools, administrative offices, medical clinics, and police posts in all parts of the district, including the most remote mountain regions. Moreover government construction crews began work on an extensive network of roads to link hitherto isolated villages with the rest of the country. A bus company initiated service to Kohistan after workers completed an unpaved road from Thull to Dir town. Travel outside Thull then became comparatively easy. Installing electricity as part of a rural electrification project, and establishing a national television channel made it possible for Kohistanis to watch reruns of "Kojak" and "Trapper John, M.D."

in hotels in Dir town. Crews strung telephone lines in many parts of the district. And in Thull, like the flu in January, *mar dushmani* swept through the network of social relationships.

The explosion of death enmity in conjunction with political and economic modernization makes organized vengeance in Thull particularly fascinating. Why would *dushmani* become focally important in Thull social relations at the same time the government politically integrated the community with the rest of Pakistan, implemented an educational system, and instituted programs of economic development? The answer lies in understanding how *dushmani* evolved in the context of changing external conditions.

The most important external change effecting *dushmani* was the construction of a transportation system linking Thull with the rest of Pakistan. It seems odd at first that a highway system would promote organized vengeance, for integrating rural communities into modern developing economic and political systems should lead to an atrophy of feuding. Yet just such an integration triggered sociocultural transitions in Thull that ultimately resulted in *dushmani*.

Following construction of the road and the establishment of regular bus service, an ever-increasing number of religious leaders from Thull traveled to Mardan and Peshawar to study in centers of Islamic learning with noted Pathan scholars and teachers. To call the version of Islam they brought back to Thull "fundamentalist" perhaps oversimplifies the new religious ideology. In any case, religious leaders introduced new concepts of honor and

The road to Thull

different notions about women that ultimately triggered the eruption of *dushmani*. Innovative ideas regarding the concept of *iman* acted as the catalyst.

Iman has two distinct but related meanings, as noted in the last chapter: "faith," and "gift" (or "blessing") from God. *Iman* as faith distinguishes Muslims from Kafirs—those who have shown a defiant ingratitude by their refusal to accept God's word and become Muslims. Kafirs are by definition cruel, immoral human beings. *Iman* as "God's gift" saves Muslims from being Kafirs, and thus from a life of evil and depravity.

What constitutes *iman* is subject to interpretation and emphasis. As we saw, all Muslims interpret *iman* to include the oneness of God and his omnipotence, the existence of special messengers who have brought God's word to mankind at various times, the existence of angels, and the belief in a day of judgment. For many Muslims, however, *iman* also includes the belief in the sanctity of saintly individuals and their power to mediate between God and man.

Saint cults were an important part of Islamic beliefs and practices in Thull before the road to Kohistan existed. The belief in saints became heresy, however, following the indoctrination of Kohistani religious leaders in fundamentalist schools of Islamic theology—schools whose doctrines denied the existence of any humans with special access to God. Religious scholars returned to their communities armed with fundamentalist theology to campaign against the belief in saints and to purify Islam. Today shrines to saints no longer exist in Thull, and Kohistanis believe *mushriks* ("believers in saints") are little better than Kafirs.

Religious leaders also argued against music and dancing (especially at weddings), and preached that secluding women was necessary to maintain men's *ghrairat* (their self integrity). This became especially important for *dushmani* because it personified the connection between male honor and the sexual purity of women. As we shall see, the situations demanding deadly retaliation consequently increased.

Once the road linked Thull to Islamic centers of learning, *ghrairat* soon replaced the belief in saints as part of Islamic faith. Today Kohistanis consider it a critical aspect of *iman*. Defining *ghrairat* as crucial to *iman* made taking vengeance a serious religious obligation, thus creating a fertile environment for *dushmani*.

The concept of *ghrairat,* as you recall, closely relates to *badal* ("revenge"), and when the *ghrairat* code became intertwined with faith, revenge became fundamental to a Muslim identity located at the core of self. We must outline the meaning of *ghrairat* once again to understand why this is so, this time juxtaposing it to *aizzat*. English speakers often translate both *ghrairat* and *aizzat* as "honor," but these concepts have distinct meanings in Kohistani thinking. *Ghrairat* is perhaps best understood as honor in the sense of personal worth, integrity, or character. *Ghrairat* is natural, a part of *iman,* and, therefore, a gift from God (in fact God's most valuable gift), as Kohistanis explain. Every Muslim is born with *ghrairat,* and a man can only lose it by failing to protect it. Others can pollute *ghrairat,* however, the way stepping in manure pollutes one's shoe.

Protecting *ghrairat* depends on following a clearly defined code of conduct. One must provide wives and daughters with appropriate food and clothing to the degree one's wealth allows; one must never permit wives and daughters to speak with men not closely related; one must never eat or exchange friendly conversation with the enemy of close paternal kin; and one must always attack those who sully one's *ghrairat.* Staring at a wife or daughter, reflecting light from a snuff box mirror on a wife or daughter, proposing intimacy with a wife or daughter, looking through a camera at a wife or daughter, fleeing or attempting to flee the community with a wife or daughter, and having illicit sexual relations with a wife or daughter sully the husband's or father's *ghrairat.* The murder of close paternal kin, verbal abuse, theft, and assault also pollute *ghrairat* and demand vengeance.

Honor in the sense of prestige best translates *aizzat.* In contrast to *ghrairat, aizzat* is artificial because the community awards it, rather than God. *Aizzat* depends on personal accomplishments and defines the men of worth in the community; it fluctuates with an individual's fortune. One measures *aizzat* by the *adab* ("respect") accorded by others. Wealth, education, piety, and elected position all merit respect and thus confer *aizzat.* Whereas a *baghrairatman* ("one without *ghrairat"*) would not be given the respect necessary for *aizzat,* losing *aizzat* does not affect *ghrairat.* If a man loses his elected position or his wealth, then he loses *aizzat,* although his *ghrairat* remains unchanged.

Political honor contrasts with moral honor in Thull. *Aizzat* is political, primarily involving politicians active in the competition for power. Hence it is vital to self for only a minority, those with political or social ambitions. *Ghrairat,* in contrast, is moral, a definitive quality in Muslim identity for all men, and relevant, potentially at least, to most male social relations. The pollution of *ghrairat* calls for revenge, so revenge too is potentially relevant to most male relationships.

The ideological connection between *ghrairat* and Islamic faith deserves further comment. Kohistani self has been rooted in Islam for centuries. Consequently, men often cast aspersions on opponents in terms of the Muslim/Kafir distinction, each accusing the other of *kafiranô kar karant* (literally, "making the work of Kafirs," that is, acting like a Kafir). Such accusations can be dangerous to health, however, because they often lead to violence and even murder. Islam is critical to self, and attacks on one's identity as a Muslim call forth such strong emotions that retaliatory violence often results. Kohistanis believe *ghrairat* to be one of the most significant elements of Islamic faith, and its defense a sacred obligation. Any act considered an attack on *ghrairat* arouses particularly strong passions usually expressed through violent retaliatory actions because it strikes at the core of self.

We can understand now why the change to a *ghrairat*-centered value system, and especially why the linking of *ghrairat* with *iman* resulted in an epidemic of death enmity. Because *ghrairat* depended so much on female sexual purity, men's identities as Muslims became vulnerable to the way other men behaved toward their women—a vulnerability dramatically increased by the wide range of actions culturally defined as polluting *ghrairat*. A glance, a word, a chance reflection of light all had potentially devastating effects on relations between men, since all could be interpreted as attacks on *ghrairat*, and all had the power to arouse strong passions for revenge. Further, the rules defining the kind of retribution demanded by *ghrairat* for different kinds of attacks significantly increased the potential for homicidal violence. Assault, theft, and even murder of close kinsmen theoretically, at least, can be settled with compensation, leaving one's self intact. Acts attacking *ghrairat* through women, in contrast, must be answered with bullets.

Ghrairat, therefore, demanded men be always wary and ready to kill in order to protect the integrity of self. At the same time, those who may have either inadvertently or purposefully acted in ways interpretable as polluting another's *ghrairat* found themselves in situations demanding constant vigilance if they were to stay alive. Hence *ghrairat* created a sea of potential enemies and placed each man squarely in the middle. That tension became pervasive in male social relationships and acid indigestion a common medical complaint, should surprise no one.

Ghrairat not only encouraged *dushmani,* but the rules defining what constituted attacks on *ghrairat* created linked sequences of reciprocal murders. If, for example, a man killed another for shining a light on his wife, then that murder cleansed his *ghrairat*. But, just as significantly, the killing polluted the *ghrairat* of the murdered man's close paternal kin, requiring them to kill in return. Consequently men developed relationships of *dushmani* both easily and often. Once developed they were difficult to end. And, finally, they were punctuated by instances of serial, retaliatory murders. The blood feud had come to Thull in full force.

Constructing the road effected economic transitions within Thull that also contributed to the growth of *dushmani*. Subsistence in Thull depended on a balance between alpine herding and agriculture during the *nawabs*' reign. The road changed all that. It made cultivating potatoes (which grow particularly well at high elevations) economically viable as a cash crop, for it allowed rapid and inexpensive trucking of produce to market centers throughout Pakistan. Furthermore it permitted farmers to cultivate more land. The number of livestock in the community limited the amount of land farmers could cultivate before the road existed because manure for animals furnished the sole source of fertilizer. Farmers could import artificial fertilizer, hence reducing their dependence on animals for manure, after the Pakistani Government had constructed the road.

Accordingly the economic base in Thull shifted from a system balanced between herding and cultivation to one weighed in favor of the cultivation of potatoes as a cash crop—a transition manifested by several changes. First, the proportion of men actively engaged in herding significantly decreased. Herding no longer provided the primary source of cash income for many families, although they continued to keep four or five goats and a few head of cattle. A significant minority of men own only a few goats, although everyone owns more than enough land for subsistence requirements. Second, an increased proportion of land came under cultivation, as herding decreased in economic importance. Farmers converted privately owned early spring pastures to more financially lucrative potato fields as they became less dependent on natural fertilizer. Third, few of those continuing to maintain large numbers of animals remained active in summer herding, preferring instead to hire shepherds from other communities.

These changes nurtured *dushmani* in two ways. First, cross-cutting ties weakened, as the proportion of men actively involved in herding diminished. Maintaining good relations with members of one's herding unit became less important for the large proportion of men no longer involved in herding activities, even though the system allocating pastures remained virtually unchanged. As crosscutting ties lost their potency in maintaining peaceful relations, *dushmani* began to flourish. Second, the change to an economic system based on cultivating potatoes as a cash crop, coupled with an increased number of fields, significantly increased hard cash in the community. The supply of money expanded even further following large scale timber exploitation, the reason the government built the road in the first place. Not only did timber contractors hire local men as wage laborers, but the government paid royalties to the community as a whole.

With increases in wealth, the number of firearms owned by members of the community increased as well; even poor men could buy rifles. Bogart's quip in *The Big Sleep,* "Such a lot of guns around town and so few brains," though perhaps a bit ethnocentric when applied to Thull, nevertheless seems appropriate. Timber royalties and potato earnings made purchasing guns easy, and men acting out emotions framed by *ghrairat* and sanctified by *iman* turned their newly purchased rifles on neighbors in a gluttony of death enmity.

Blood feuding in Thull developed only recently, occurring within a historical context shaped by economic change and political modernization. It can best be understood as the result of two interrelated developments: First, a transition to an ideological system in which *ghrairat* became a critical component in the construction of Muslim identity and, second, a transition from a subsistence system based on herding and cultivation to an economic system built on timbering and cash crop agriculture. The key to understanding why these transitions generated *dushmani* lies in grasping the consequences of particular changes that were a part of the larger transitions. Linking *ghrairat* to *iman* injected revenge into Muslim identity and made revenge emotions critical to the integrity of self, whereas economic development made possible the spread of modern firearms. Together these factors encouraged, and perhaps even required, organized vengeance within the community.

5 / The Distortion of Ecology and Economics

Natural environments do not produce sociocultural arrangements. Death enmity in Thull cannot be mechanically derived from the jagged mountains and broken valleys that gave the community birth. But if the violence of the land does not create the violence of its people, how does the particular way the Kohistanis of Thull exploit their environment relate to *dushmani?* We must turn the question around to answer it, inverting our perspective. I discussed *dushmani* in the passive voice in the last chapter, asking how it was affected by historical transformations. Now I will frame it in the active voice, focusing on *dushmani*'s consequences for the way people in Thull relate to natural resources.

Why bother with involved descriptions of how people make a living? What is significant about an irrigation system, for example, that warrants a detailed account? By looking beneath the seemingly monotonous litany of ethnographic detail, we can identify general features, although the minutiae have little significance in themselves. How the blood feud relates to these general features can then be understood. Blood feuding directly affects some of the ways people use resources, whereas it affects others only obliquely. Nevertheless it ultimately affects all in some way. Accordingly I begin by depicting physical surroundings, then discuss land use patterns, and finally describe the effects of *dushmani.*

THE NATURAL ENVIRONMENT

Getting to Thull is no small task. The road leads across the Indus River to the foot of the Hindu-Kush Mountains, and then climbs the switchbacks of the Malakand Pass to Chakdarra. Near here a small contingent of British soldiers (including a young Winston Churchill) fought 6000 Pathan tribesmen in the Ysufzai uprising of 1901. From Chakdarra the road winds up the Panjkora Valley to Dir town, the market and administrative center for Dir Kohistan. The road is paved to Dir Town, but Thull lies some forty miles beyond at the end of a dirt road impassable in bad weather. The main settlement lies at approximately 7000 feet of elevation. The community owns roughly 40 kilometers of territory stretching along the Panjkora Valley, including land for fields and summer pastures.

The mountains of Thull

Those hazarding the trip to Thull find a bleak, but nonetheless beautiful, landscape at their journey's end. Houses cluster at the foot of towering peaks (reaching as high as 15,000 feet) or scatter here and there on lonely outcrops and hidden plateaus. A tangled mass of crags broods over land littered with smashed boulders, severed by swift running streams, and periodically shattered by the growing pains of mountains whose convulsions occasionally destroy the top of the Richter scale. Throughout the valleys and mountains humans cultivate thin, sandy-colored soil where the terrain permits, and pasture their herds on fairway-smooth meadows bordering the Panjkora's edge and strewn high among mammoth evergreen forests. The Panjkora Valley widens within the confines of Thull's boundaries, thus permitting the cultivation of land adjacent to the river's edge without building complex systems of stone terrace walls and irrigation channels. Most fields, however, are located away from the river on mountain slopes, where the terrain requires extensive terracing, unfortunately for the farmers of Thull. Ancient builders constructed most terraced walls to 3 or 4 feet in height from loose stones carefully chosen to fit tightly together. They date from pagan times some three hundred years ago, according to local traditions.

IRRIGATION

Thull enjoys relatively plentiful rain and snow. Snow sometimes accumulates to 6 feet at the valley floor, amassing to much greater depths in the mountains. Runoff from melting snow provides a major source of the

Terraced fields

Panjkora's water. The high mountain peaks wring moisture from the air throughout the early spring, helping seeds to germinate. In 1984, for example, rain fell every day from April 24th through May 17th. So much rain and snow fall in some years that the Panjkora ravages the land with destructive spring floods, destroying fields and washing away houses, livestock, and even people. In late summer, monsoon showers provide an additional source of moisture, drenching the land.

Nevertheless from late May to mid-August nature provides so little rainfall that crops growing in fields away from the Panjkora require periodic watering. Of the staple crops, maize must be irrigated six or seven times a season, whereas potatoes require watering three or four times a summer. The condition of the leaves on plants tells the farmer when his fields need watering, a task accomplished by a complex system of irrigation channels (see Figure 3). Channel headworks are simple enough, consisting of rocks and boulders piled into a rough wall. Headworks extend into the river about 5 feet, diverting river water to the irrigation ditches. From the headworks, located in Kumrats, an area of meadows to the north of Thull Proper. The ditches lead down the valley, but at an incline less than that of the river. Wooden viaducts span chasms and hug cliffs when necessary. After extending down the valley to the beginning of Thull's southern boundary, a distance of some 15 kilometers, irrigation channels cut into mountain slopes far above the valley floor. Here the irrigation ditches bring water to fields high in the mountains, hundreds of feet above the river's elevation. Subsidiary channels direct water from main channels to the fields below. Kohistanis call their irrigated fields *neheri,* the channels themselves *neher.* Landowners must keep in repair the subsidiary channels that feed water to their fields, in addition to the main channels bordering their land. Those benefiting from them maintain together the main channels watering fields owned by more than one person.

Irrigation water is usually so plentiful that farmers divert water into their fields whenever necessary. However, high in the mountains, where water must be transported long distances, a substantial amount is either absorbed into the bottom of the irrigation ditches or lost through evaporation,

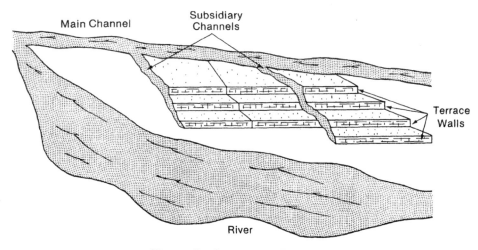

Figure 3   Irrigation System

necessitating a systems of turns. Fields at the highest point on a mountain slope get the morning turn; those at the middle point, the afternoon turn; and those at the lowest location must be irrigated in the evening. During dry years water can be so scarce that irrigation disputes sometimes explode between the owners of neighboring fields, often resulting in physical violence and even murder. Some farmland needs no irrigation, for moisture seeps from underneath the ground, providing a constant source of water. All such land, called *jelgal* in Kohistani, is immediately adjacent to the river near Thull Proper.

AGRICULTURE

Potatoes (*akur*) and maize (*jawal*) form the two staple crops in Thull, but most farmers also grow vegetables (spinach, tomatoes, and beans) in small gardens close to their homes. Orchard trees abound, most planted near houses so that owners can protect the yield from thieves. Apple, peach, cherry, apricot, mulberry, and walnut grow particularly well in Thull's cool mountain climate. People also collect wild greens, berries, and mushrooms in the high mountain pastures to vary the diet.

Plowing commences during the last week in April and continues throughout May at Thull's elevation. Those fortunate enough to own *jelgal* fields adjacent to the river generally plow with rented tractors transported

Plowing jelgal *fields*

from Dir town, although a few wealthy individuals in Thull own tractors themselves. Most men, however, use the kind of ox-drawn plow found throughout the Hindu-Kush. The plow is made of wood, its plowshare sometimes covered with metal. Plowing a field of average size usually requires the labor of two to three men working in shifts. The men of Thull measure fields not by their size, but by the time required to plow them. They call the unit of measurement an *aide*. One *aide* measures the amount of land that a man can plow by oxen once in a day, and by tractor twice in an hour. Elders in Thull devised this system of measurement because the contours of fields are so irregular that one can calculate field size by area only with difficulty.

Farmers plow both maize and potato fields at about the same time, from late April through the end of May. They plow fields planted with maize twice. After the initial plowing, women sow maize seed by hand, using a broadcast method; then men plow the field again to bury the seed. When the plants reach about 6 inches in height, women transplant those growing too close together. Men then fertilize and irrigate the fields. When the plants reach about 4 feet in height, women remove whatever weeds are interfering with the crop.

Women harvest maize. They cut off the stalk and then carry the cut stalks to their rooftops for threshing. The ears are picked from the stalks by hand and placed in the sun to dry. Each stalk normally yields two ears between 4 to 8 inches in length. The stalks are stored for winter fodder. When the ears dry enough to loosen the kernels, the women beat them from the ears with wooden sticks. They place the kernels in the sun again, and when they

A wooden plow

A water-powered mill

dry, men bag and carry them to one of the many water-driven mills, where a miller grinds them into corn meal.

Potatoes require considerably more labor than maize. After ox-drawn plows (or tractors, as the case may be) cut the fields into furrows, women break the large clumps of earth that remain with a hoe-like implement, a back-breaking and time-consuming task. Men, working in teams of two, mold the loose soil into square-shaped mounds with a *chare*. A *chare* is roughly the same size and shape as the ordinary garden spade but differs in some important respects. The cutting blade is longer and narrower than the garden spade, with almost no curve. A few inches above the blade a cross-bar about 6 inches long intersects the shaft. Two pieces of rope about 4 feet long are tied to the ends of the crossbar; the other ends of the rope connect to a wooden handle. One man holds the shaft and exerts force with a forward motion. His helper faces him, and, at the same time his partner pushes the *chare* forward, he exerts force by pulling the handle connected to the cross-bar by the two pieces of rope.

While *chare* teams mound the soil, girls cut seedling potatoes into small pieces, each containing at least one eye. Teams of boys then plant the pieces into the sides of the mounds. Finally, the men depress the center of each mound with the *chare* to hold moisture. Farmers fertilize and irrigate the fields when plants reach about 2 inches in height. Men irrigate their fields as needed throughout the growing season, based on the condition of the plants. Women weed whenever necessary.

Potatoes require four to five months to mature. Hence, the potato harvest begins sometime between late September and early October. Men and women working together harvest the crop, digging the potatoes from the earth with a scythe-like implement. The women's version is short-handled, a little over 2 feet in length, as women usually work in a squatting position. The men's version is longer (about 4 feet in length). The average-sized field yields roughly 40 sacks of potatoes.

Agriculture in Thull possesses a dualistic quality, torn between cash crop and subsistence farming. Family units consume the maize, vegetables, and fruit they produce themselves, whereas farmers grow potatoes primarily to sell in down-country markets. Although potatoes grow particularly well in Thull, they require more fertilizer than farmers can produce using traditional methods—mixing animal dung with decomposed leaves. Consequently the potato crop depends on chemical fertilizer that farmers must purchase with cash at markets located in neighboring communities. Men usually spend one or two days purchasing and transporting chemical fertilizer to Thull.

After the potato harvest, the crop must be trucked to lowland markets in Peshawar, the capital of the Northwest Frontier Province. An average-sized truck transports approximately 100 sacks of potatoes, so if a man harvests a large crop he usually rents a truck himself. Most men, however, share the cost of truck rentals with a partner chosen on a purely utilitarian basis. Whoever owns a crop bagged and ready to ship joins with someone in a similar position to share rental costs. Anyone will suffice as a partner, except a *dushman*.

Usually farmers try to increase their profits by taking advantage of market conditions, timing their shipment to coincide with market scarcity. Those with kin living in Peshawar hold an advantage, because they can provide information about market conditions. Yet potato prices fluctuate rapidly and dramatically. Sometimes farmers find the price of potatoes so low when their crop reaches market that they cannot recover fertilizer and truck rental costs.

Kohistani farmers living in communities at lower elevations in the Panjkora Valley grow two crops during the year, winter wheat and maize. Pathan farmers grow rice as well in the valley below Dir town. Recently small shops have proliferated in Thull selling wheat and rice grown in these neighboring communities. They sell an endless assortment of junk (plastic sandals, matches, kerosene, soap, combs, snuff, and cheap toys) as well. As a result Thull has become integrated into an economic system wider than the community itself.

HERDING

Thull augments agriculture with a kind of alpine pastoralism found throughout the Hindu-Kush region. Unlike other mountain communities in the Hindu-Kush, however, the economic system in Thull no longer balances between farming and herding. In the last few decades agriculture has come to weigh more heavily in the economy than animal husbandry. Only a few of the approximately 2500 men in Thull own herds of more than a hundred animals, and less than half own herds larger than ten. Many families keep only one or two goats. Goats constitute most animals in Kohistani herds, although some men do own cows and water buffalo as well. Donkeys and horses provide the primary means of transporting supplies to and from mountain pastures.

Kohistanis practice a form of vertical transhumance. Those with large numbers of animals keep them in barns located near permanent settlements during the winter months. Most people, however, quarter the few animals they own in specially constructed rooms beneath their houses. Animals forage in pastures close to settlements in the early spring. Although private citizens own early spring pastures, men can graze their animals wherever they wish, so long as the pastures do not belong to their *dushmans*. The men of Thull generally prefer their animals to graze on land they own, because the animals fertilize the fields with their manure.

Herd owners must take their animals into the mountains after fields have been planted in the spring to protect seedling crops from damage. Goats in particular forage voraciously, and if large numbers remained close to settlements, they would destroy crops in nearby fields. Village elders decide when herds must be taken to the mountain pastures, usually sometime in early June. Every family in the community can keep at least one animal at home throughout the summer to provide milk for its needs. Each day a shepherd takes all the animals that remain in the settlement area to community-owned pastures in the mountains close to Thull specifically reserved for

Early summer pastures

this purpose; he returns them to the homes of their owners each evening. The owners of the animals contribute a portion of milk to the shepherd in return for his labor.

Thull owns most summer pastures in common and each spring allocates them by lottery to groups called *lud*s. I must briefly outline how descent groups organize themselves for us to understand how the lottery operates, although I shall discuss descent in greater detail in the next chapter. The people of Thull are divided into three patrilineal clans, each composed of several patrilineages. Patrilineages from all three clans group together to form twelve different *lud*s. While *lud*s are not descent groups, that is, all the members of a particular *lud* do not trace descent from a common ancestor, each *lud* takes its name from one of its component patrilineages. Thus, for example, in 1984 the Hasanor *lud* comprised the Hasanor, Mulnor, Chetior, Kayor, and Ijior patrilineages. Of these, the Hasanor and Chetior make up parts of the Miror clan, the Mulnor and Kayor are in the Meskol clan, and the Ijior comprises a section of the Silor clan. *Lud* membership, therefore, cross-cuts clans, a significant feature of the system, as I discussed earlier. Moreover, the elders of the community can change the component patrilineages of *lud* from year to year to balance their size and minimize overgrazing.

Also to minimize overgrazing, the summer pastures of Thull are divided into two areas, the first only usable in the early summer, and the second in the late summer. Each of these is further subdivided into territorial units

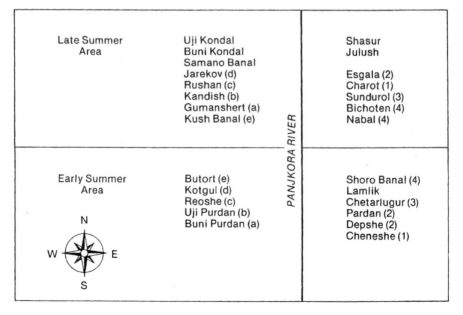

Figure 4   A schematic map of the banals *of Thull. Numbers and letters in parentheses show paired relationships. Individuals in the community own those* banals *with no numbers or letters after their names.*

called *banal*s. *Banal*s consist of pastures, animal pens, and huts located within their confines.

Specific *banal*s in the early summer grazing area are linked to ones in the late summer grazing area for purposes of the lottery. Thus, for example, Buni Purdan, a *banal* in the early summer grazing area couples with Gumanshert in the late summer grazing area. Sometimes two *banal*s combine with only one in the counterpart area because of their small size. Depshe and Pardan in the early summer area together pair with Esgala, a *banal* in the late summer area. Thull owns in common twenty *banal*s, whereas private individuals in the community own six (see Figure 4).

All interested parties in Thull gather in the spring to allocate *banal*s among the various *lud*s by lottery. The meeting always takes place on Torwalo Shan, the large rooftop where the men of Thull hold many of their public gatherings. Herd owners held the lottery on June 10th in 1984. Most animals had passed through the two wooden gates located on either side of the Panjkora River by June 14th. These gates mark the boundary between the areas of summer pastures and the rest of the community.

The lottery works as follows: Each *lud* owns a particular symbol which is carved onto a short stick about 6 inches long. Elders place the sticks into a hat and choose a small boy (because young children are allegedly impartial) to draw the sticks from the hat. The community allocates to the *lud* owning the symbol on the first stick drawn the southernmost *banal* on the east side of the Panjkora River (in addition to its linked *banal* in the late summer grazing area). The next drawing allocates the most southern *banal* on the west side of the river (and its linked *banal*). For example, if the boy first drew the stick with the Hasanor symbol carved on it, the members of the Hasanor *lud* must graze their herds in Cheneshe and Charot. The next stick he drew would allocate Buni Purdan and Gumanshert to the *lud* whose symbol was carved on that particular stick (note number and letter labels in Figure 4). The lottery would continue until the drawing distributed all the *banal*s among the various *lud*s.

Most herd owners prefer to spend summers working in potato fields near their homes than with their animals in distant mountain pastures. Accordingly they hire shepherds to do that work if possible. Most hired shepherds come from the Gujar community in Gwaldai, a side valley of the Panjkora near Dir Town. Gujars are a gypsylike ethnic group that have spread throughout the Hindu-Kush mountains during the last three centuries. Most Gujars remain nomadic today, moving from the lowlands of Malakand to the high mountains of Kohistan. Some, however, conquered territory from earlier inhabitants or settled permanently on vacant land. Gujars speak an Indic language and most probably originated in Punjab.

The people of Thull believe that Gujars make superb shepherds. They allegedly take better care of animals than do Kohistanis because of their legendary love for goats. Still, most Gujars prefer to herd their own animals. Consequently a herd owner must sometimes hire a poor man from Thull, arrange for kinsmen to do the work, or shepherd the animals himself. One

A shepherd's hut

shepherd usually herds 120 animals for a six-month season. He receives rps.1000 (roughly $750) for his labor. The work itself includes tending the herds, milking the animals, and making cheese and ghee (clarified butter) from the milk products.

LUMBERING

Any account of economic activities in Thull must mention lumbering, as Kohistanis are obsessed with protecting their timber rights. Communities in Dir Kohistan have periodically fought one another over conflicting claims to timber resources in recent years. In 1985 a full-scale war over conflicting claims broke out in Dogdarra, a side valley of the Panjkora about 20 miles from Thull. Enemy villages used automatic rifles, machine guns, and rocket launchers against one another in fierce fighting. Pakistani Government troops finally blockaded the road from Thull to Dir town to pressure the opposing sides to make peace. Kalkot and Piar, two Kohistani communities close to Thull, have fought over ownership of forests for the past twenty years. During the waning years of Ali Bhutto's rule, Kohistani and Pathan communities in Dir united in armed insurrection against the Pakistani Army over the government's timber policy. Local communities fought so fiercely that Pakistani commanders called in air strikes and deployed tanks against the rebels. Many died before mediators from outside the valley resolved the dispute. They convinced the government to increase timber royalties to the local communities, which ended the fighting.

Now the government department in charge of exploiting timber resources awards contracts to timber contractors from Thull to deliver an agreed-upon number of logs each year. Contractors hire local lumberjacks to cut down trees, and arrange for trucks to transport logs to the community timber depot at Ajishe, near Thull's southern boundary. Government-hired truckers transport the logs from Ajishe to a depot near the mouth of the Panjkora in southern Dir. The government pays the contractor a set fee, and he recompenses his lumberjacks from these proceeds. Additionally the government disburses annual royalties to Thull based on the number of logs delivered and the average price of timber during that year. Then the men of Thull select a trusted individual to equitably divide royalties at a public meeting. The head of each family in Thull received rps.15,000 (about $1000) from timber royalties in 1983.

ECONOMICS

We can reduce the details of economics in Thull to three general features most affected by *dushmani:* Men devote more effort to growing potatoes than herding goats; women take most of the responsibility for growing and harvesting maize; and men fight for their forests. The most important principles of economic life in Thull—the discontinuity between subsistence and cash-related activities, and the weight given the cash side of the economic equation—lie beneath these features.

That Kohistanis would be (and perhaps should be) preoccupied with making money is self-evident to Americans. Does not everyone wish to better themselves by increasing their purchasing power? What would we do without ever-increasing cash? We could not send our children to elite colleges whose tuitions increase annually. We could not buy that beautiful new BMW or Camaro every three years. And most appalling, we would have to stop, or at best curtail, shopping at our favorite mall. But in Thull, malls do not exist, and a year's timber royalties for only a few families equal the yearly trade of all the stores in town. Thull has no electricity, so buying television sets, computers, or state-of-the-art audio systems would be useless. Thull has no streets, so buying that new BMW would not demonstrate rational economic behavior. Furthermore, more people build houses themselves than purchase them, and more produce the food they eat than buy it. Most women weave wool and sew the cloth for their family's coats; no one buys them at Sak's Fifth Avenue. If consumer goods exist only in limited quantities (and are not vital to economic life in any case) and people produce most of the necessities of life themselves, why does economic activity skew toward acquiring cash? If all one can do with money is hoard it, why care so much about earning it?

Although food, drink, shelter, and clothing require only minimal sums of money, staying alive in Thull does require major outlays of cash for most men. Money might not buy much, but it does buy guns; men may not care about owning that shiny new Camaro, but they love trips to the gun bazaar in Bajour to pick out that shiny new Kalashnikov (AK-47) assault rifle. And once they own it, like Americans with a new car, they itch to try it.

ECONOMIC CHANGE

In the last chapter we examined how political modernization and economic development helped initiate *dushmani*. Once born, *dushmani* itself affected economic activities. As it spread through the weave of social relationships, owning guns became a question of life or death. More sophisticated, but significantly more expensive, weapons became available following the Soviet invasion of neighboring Afghanistan because Afghan resistance fighters brought captured Russian weapons across the border to sell in Pakistan. An arms race began in Thull as men sought to better, or at least match, the fire power of their enemies with more sophisticated weapons of their own. Understandably they required increasing amounts of money to purchase the more expensive weapons needed to remain competitive. Thus the economic balance tilted in favor of activities producing cash. Potato farming and timbering became critically important to men, leaving to women much of the work necessary to grow maize; Gujars were hired to guard the herds.

Economic development, therefore, may have played midwife to the birth of death enmity, but as it waxed in importance, *dushmani* itself intensified the processes of economic modernization. The new economic system it helped create weighted cash cropping more heavily than subsistance, which in turn made economics in Thull more sensitive to forces outside the community. *Dushmani* powered the integration of Thull into a wider, more modern economic system by tilting the economic balance toward a cash crop economy and in the process strengthened the forces breaking down community barriers.

The consequences of *dushmani* are not limited to agriculture and herding, but touch in some way all aspects of the way people in Thull relate to the land. The list is too long to discuss in its entirety, but it includes several examples interesting, diverse, and strange enough to discuss in detail. These range from shelters and settlement patterns to the places used to perform basic bodily functions and the domesticated animals people keep.

REVENGE AND THE STRUCTURE OF HOUSES

The men of Thull build houses differently than people in neighboring valleys, where blood feuding is not so entrenched in the socioeconomic system. The floor plan in Figure 5 shows several features of contemporary

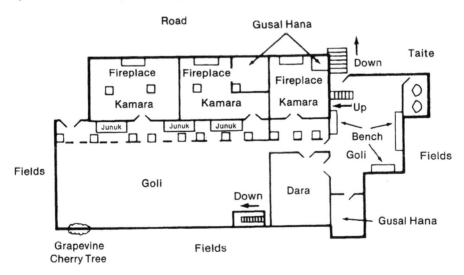

Goli - Courtyard
Dara - Guest Room
Kamar - Family Living Room
□ - Post

Taite - Latrine
Gusal Hana - Bath Area
Junuk - Storage Chest

Figure 5   Floor Plan of Contemporary Kohistani House

houses in Thull. First, the builder organized the house around two partially enclosed courtyards; one enters through a gate leading to the male-dominated, outer part of the house. Benches line three sides of that courtyard, and friends gather there to sit in the sun and exchange gossip in good weather. The men of the house invite their guests into the men's guest room if the weather is too cool to sit comfortably in the open. The men's guest room has two doors. One opens to the courtyard, while the other leads to the inner, more intimate part of the house, that space in which women move freely about their work, unhindered by the black scarf that covers their face when unrelated men are present. Hosts bring their male guests food and tea prepared by women through this door. Women never enter the outer, public part of the house when guests are present, nor do unrelated men enter the inner area. Additional doors open to the men's bath area and to a latrine from the outer courtyard.

Thick walls and a stout door separate the outer from the inner courtyard. Living rooms occupied by each of the owners (three brothers) and their families face this courtyard. Bathing areas (but no latrines) for women are located in corners of the living rooms, and chests for storing grain line their outside walls. Fireplaces that draw smoke poorly at best provide heat for the living rooms in winter. A trap door in the courtyard's floor opens to a ladder leading to an enclosed area housing cows and goats during the winter months.

Although not all recently built houses in Thull follow identical floor plans, they do share basic principles in layout which differentiate the houses of Thull from those in other regions of the Hindu-Kush where blood feuding does not organize social relations. First, barriers divide outer areas where women cannot go when male strangers are present from inner sections forbidden to unrelated men. Second, men use latrines attached to houses, but women must defecate in hidden corners of fields after dark. Third, bathing areas for women are located in the most secluded parts of houses. Fourth, fireplaces with enclosed chimneys heat houses in Thull, rather than open hearths whose smoke escapes through holes in roofs. And, finally, men often build houses in Thull with no windows.

Separating houses into outer, male-dominated, and inner, female-dominated areas exemplifies *purdah*. In an earlier chapter I discussed how *purdah* exhibits honor and how honor affects *dushmani*. Thus physically separating male and female parts of houses is one component in the complex of beliefs and practices expressing *purdah*, honor, and *dushmani*.

Given *purdah* we can also understand that bathing areas for women are located in the most secluded parts of houses. But why, then, would builders locate latrines in public parts of houses, while requiring women to relieve themselves in fields where they are more exposed to outsiders? The reason is simple. Most murders occur at night, and men are never more vulnerable than when an enemy catches them in the dark with their pants down. Women can safely defecate in fields adjacent to their homes because men cannot see them and *dushman*s cannot kill them for revenge. Were men to use fields for that purpose, however, they would put themselves at considerable

A contemporary house

risk. Accordingly, men build latrines attached to their houses to protect themselves against their enemies, as they freely acknowledge. Interestingly enough, latrines do not exist in neighboring communities where *dushmani* is not so pervasive. There, cornfields are everyone's toilet.

The men of Thull do not build houses with fireplaces and chimneys in place of the more traditional open hearths and smoke holes for their increased heating efficiency. Chimneys are so poorly designed in Thull that they draw smoke no better than the smoke holes of more traditional Hindu-Kush houses. Furthermore, open hearths located in the middle of rooms provide more heat than enclosed fireplaces positioned on back walls. Smoke holes, however, have a serious disadvantage over fireplaces in the struggle to stay alive. Enemies can creep onto the roof of a house under the cover of darkness and shoot their unsuspecting victims through the smoke hole. Enclosed fireplaces and chimneys, in contrast, protect against this threat by taking away clear lines of fire. Similarly men build houses without windows so that *dushman* cannot shoot through them at those inside the house.

Old houses, those in Thull Proper where residences are packed tightly together, originally resembled buildings located throughout the Hindu-Kush in structure and organization. Recent owners, however, have extensively renovated the old houses, covering smoke holes and windows, constructing fireplaces and chimneys, erecting latrines, building courtyards, and creating separate inner and outer sections.

Yet such efforts have met with only partial success, for the structure of the original buildings limits the possible changes. Adding latrines to old houses poses especially difficult problems because in situating houses original builders did not take into account how to dispose of accumulated human waste. Thus many latrines in Thull Proper must be cleaned every few days, unlike those of more recently built houses. All too often, renovating houses takes on a Rube Goldberg quality because the structural changes require so many compromises. Moreover, houses in Thull Proper stand on various levels of an old river terrace, so that one gains access to the roofs of most houses relatively easily from the house above. Men must guard against enemies jumping down onto their roof in the dark, chopping through the covered smoke hole, and shooting them as they sleep.

Accordingly many men abandon their houses in Thull Proper and move to the surrounding countryside; in the process they considerably alter settlement patterns in the community. They build their new houses to frustrate attackers, scattering them in locations far from unrelated neighbors; surrounding them with open fields and clear lines of rifle fire, and constructing them with built-in latrines and no windows. Death enmity is killing the classic Hindu-Kush compact settlement pattern in Thull.

DOGS AND VENGEANCE

Finally, attitudes toward domesticated animals—dogs in particular—distinguish Thull from most other Hindu-Kush communities where blood feuding is unimportant. Muslims generally despise dogs because they eat feces, which makes them unclean animals according to Islamic beliefs. People either kick, stone, or ignore them in most mountain villages in the Hindu-Kush. Usually these dogs must forage for food, for their owners rarely feed them. Most men in Thull, however, treat dogs differently, considering them particularly valuable animals. Owners worry about their health and feed them religiously. The most valuable dogs in Thull are a kind originally bred by Gujars to protect their herds from rustlers. Many men in Thull own them, especially if they have enemies, for these are frightening animals, larger and more vicious than junkyard dogs in the United States.

Owners keep their Gujar dogs chained close to the doors of their houses during the day and let them loose to roam the fields surrounding their houses at night. One can walk at night without fear of the dogs as long as one stays on boundary paths. Gujar dogs never stray across the outer boundaries of their owner's fields. Were one foolish enough to leave the path, however, the dogs would launch a fatal onslaught. Men find attacking their enemies' houses without shooting the dogs (which destroys the element of surprise) a difficult, if not impossible task, especially in darkness. Hence dogs possess value as defensive weapons rather than pets. The men of Thull care for them in much the same way they care for their rifles. As Makhbul explained, one knows the number and strength of a man's *dushmans* by the number of dogs he keeps. Gujar dogs seem to overrun Thull.

6 / The Unbalancing
of Kinship

Dushmani skewed economics in Thull, significantly changing the balance between herding and agriculture. Similarly death enmity disrupted kinship, reorganizing the relationship between its group and network dimensions. Kinship and politics intertwine in Thull, and *dushmani* effected changes in kinship through its impact on politics. The structure of kinship relationships does not determine politics in Thull, however. On the contrary, it frames it. Consequently I do not discuss the intricacies of Kohistani kinship here but concentrate on aspects that specifically relate to politics.

The political relevancy of kinship in Thull begins with what A.R. Radcliffe-Brown, one of the founding fathers of social anthropology, called the principle of the equivalence of siblings. Few modern-day anthropologists think about human actions as expressing social structural principles. Nevertheless this idea helps us understand how people in Thull conceptualize the relationship among groups of brothers and sisters. Whatever disagreements brothers might have among themselves, everyone else expects them to present a united front to outsiders, almost as if they were a single person. Correspondingly, Kohistanis sometimes think of brothers as if they were interchangeable, one the social equivalent of the others. Thus a man can even a score by taking revenge on the brother of an enemy if, for some reason, he cannot touch the enemy himself.

Kohistanis categorize brothers differently than do Americans. *Ja*, the Kohistani word for brother, refers not only to a male sharing the same father but one sharing the same paternal grandfather as well. Kohistanis think that all males descended through men from a common ancestor are brothers in a sense, and unified as a group against outsiders. These males form part of what anthropologists call a patrilineal descent group (females also belong to such groups) and what the people of Thull call a *dum*.

Descent group organization forms an important dimension of kinship in Thull. Before blood feuding claimed center stage in social relationships, it provided the most important frame for politics in the community. This is no longer the case, for death enmity weakened the political significance of descent; at the same time it strengthened the political importance of kinship networks. To understand how blood feuding changed the balance between kinship dimensions we must first understand the dimensions themselves.

75

Accordingly I begin with descent group organization and then consider kinship networks.

DESCENT GROUP ORGANIZATION

Thull divides into three major descent groups or clans, called in Kohistani *gan dums* (*gan* meaning "big"). The clans divide into twenty-two minor descent groups, or lineages, called *lukut dums* (*lukut* meaning "small"). The suffix *-or* pluralizes clan and lineage names (see Figure 6). Thus, for example, Kohistanis call the descendants of Key the Keyor and the descendants of Hasan the Hasanor, just as Americans might refer to the descendants of John Smith as "the Smiths." Sometimes people use *Khel* as the pluralizer, from Pushto (the language of the Pathans). For example, people in Thull often call the Mulnor lineage of the Meskol clan the Mullah Khel. This is because its members trace descent from the Pathan mullah who came to live in Thull soon after the people there became Muslims.

The descent groups themselves form part of an organizational framework called a segmentary system by anthropologists. The principle behind segmentary systems, called segmentary opposition, is simple. Tribal people express it in a proverb known in various forms throughout the Middle East and Southwest Asia: "Me against my brother, me and my brother against my cousin, me, my brother, and my cousin against the world." In other words, people belong to nesting series of groups in segmentary systems. Which particular group emerges at any given time is relative. In Figure 7, all those descended from John form a descent group, but only relative to those descended from Jim. The Jims and the Johns together form a group as the descendants of Harry, but again, only relative to the Hanks. And the Harrys and the Hanks form a group as the descendants of Mike relative to outsiders. In classic segmentary systems people at lower levels of segmentation put aside their disputes and unite against opponents at higher levels whenever those rivals pose serious dangers. Yet disputes which divide lower-level groups become relevant again when the threats posed by opponents at higher levels of the system disappear. Although enmity and alliance constantly fluctuate, the pattern of change is predictable, because the structure of the system itself determines the organization of alliances and oppositions.

Figure 6   Thull Clans and Their Component Lineages

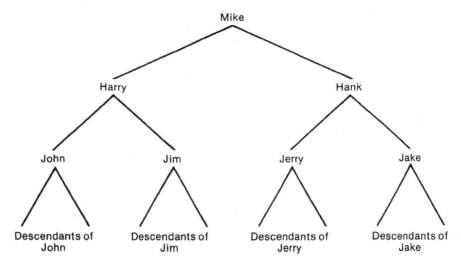

Figure 7   *An Idealized Segmentary Lineage System*

Kinship groups in Thull do not constitute as neat a system. Nevertheless the general principle holds—but, as we shall see, only roughly. At the apex of the system stands the *qaom.* Kohistanis use this word for groups distinct from others because they hold common territories and share common kinship. *Qaom,* therefore, roughly means community. Among those living within the boundaries of Thull—for example, those who can buy and sell land; those who can own houses; and, most importantly today, those who share timber royalties—constitute the *qaom.* They refer to themselves as *thullowal,* the people of Thull, and most find their marriage partners within this group. Thus kinship creates tightly interwoven networks of social relations within each *qaom.* The *qaom,* in turn, divides into constituent clans and lineages. The communities, the clans (*gan dum*s) and lineages (*lukut dum*s) are enduring segmentary units in Kohistani social organization.

Kohistanis also recognize a fourth level of segmentation in some instances. They sometimes call by the name of a common ancestor sets of close agnatic kin (people related through males) that have many members because of accidents of birth and death. Thus the numerous children, paternal grandchildren, and paternal great grandchildren of Akbar Shah Malik, an influential elder of the Chetior lineage, will be called the Akbaror after his death, according to some in Thull. Whether his descendants achieve the status of *lukut dum* ("lineage") in subsequent years will depend on their maintaining political unity in the affairs of the community. Most groups like the Akbaror lose political cohesiveness after a few generations, and people forget their names. But some do not, and in the past they have become new *lukut dum*s, replacing lineages that no longer operated effectively as political units because of shrunken membership. The process was gradual, taking place over many generations.

The Akbaror

THE POLITICS OF SEGMENTATION

Anthropologists argue whether segmentary opposition organizes politics in a mechanical fashion. Do the members of a lineage unite against members of other lineages, do the component lineages of a clan unite against other clans, and does the community unite against outsiders? The men of Thull stated unequivocally that they do, and offered the following account to illustrate how lineages and clans unite against outside threats.

The Mulnor lineage of the Meskol clan and the Hajior lineage of the Silor clan gathered each spring for a feast in Kumrat. This is an area of open pastures and forests close to Thull Proper, the community's core settlement. One spring (around the year 1965) some men of the Miror clan announced their intention to participate in the fun. Unfortunately, as it turned out, the Mulnor and the Hajior categorically refused to allow them to join their party.

On the morning of the feast, Hajior and Mulnor *maliks* ("leaders") collected the animals they planned to slaughter, mounted their horses, and rode to Kumrat. When they arrived, about five Miror men attacked them with clubs and stones from hidden positions in the forest. The attackers badly beat the *maliks* and drove the animals into the mountains, although they killed no one. When word of the beatings reached Thull Proper, a wild melee erupted. First, the fight opposed the Hajior and Mulnor lineages against the Miror but soon spread to all the lineages of the Silor and Meskol clans against the united lineages of the Miror. The battle lasted a day. Even young boys took part in the fighting—and with great enthusiasm, according to some who participated as youths. Anwar, a member of the Meskol clan and ten years old at the time, hit Shah Hajji on the head with a stone as he sought refuge under a tree. Anwar told me the story with great relish, particularly because Shah Hajji is now a powerful, but long-winded and rather pompous, Miror *malik.*

Other stories relate how Thull unites to fight other communities and how lineages oppose other lineages. Yet segmentary opposition can only account for general features of political alliances among kinship groups. For example, knowing the segmentary structure of Thull clans will not help us predict whether the Meskol will ally with the Silor or Miror. Similarly, segmentary opposition cannot tell us much about alliances between lineages within clans. If the Biror lineage of the Miror clan were to fight the Hasanor lineage of that clan, segmentary opposition cannot determine the allegiances of the other lineages because they are all situated at the same level of segmentation.

As sources for models of segmentary opposition, the stories also mislead because Thull politics do not always oppose kin groups. Consequently, segmentary opposition has limited impact on politics in many instances. An understanding of the real significance of segmentary opposition requires knowing when and how membership in kinship groups is germane. This leads back to the rivalry between the Miror and Silor clans. The row over who could go to whose parties (which in a telling way resembles squabbles among Dr. Seuss' Sneetches over hotdog roasts) was one event in a long rivalry between the Silor and Miror. The antagonism has its roots in the community's founding, according to local tradition.

The myth of Thull's founding—and the beginning of the rivalry—is worth repeating. Although in all probability the myth does not contain accurate historical details, the rival versions of the myth express basic cultural principles that organize Kohistani experience in a variety of circumstances.

First, the Silor version.

Many years ago two *Kafir* brothers, Sil and Chor, lived with their families in the upper Panjkora River Valley. When the great Muslim saint Akund Salak Baba came to the area now belonging to Thull, he found Sil camped on the east bank of the river. After listening to the wise preaching of the great saint, Sil embraced Islam. His brother, however, would not listen to the word of God and instead retreated with his followers to a fortress cave in the mountains. The cave could only be entered after climbing a long ladder, since its mouth was high on the face of a small cliff. Chor pulled the ladder into the cave behind him and prepared for a long siege. Finally, Sil captured his brother by luring him from the cave with promises of food, and brought him in chains to Akund Salak Baba. Chor could refuse to embrace Islam no longer. The great saint gave him the name Amir, or Mir, after Chor said the words of the *Kalima* that made him Muslim. From that time hence the descendants of Sil and Mir, the Silor and Miror clans, were rivals.

The version of the myth told by Miror men contains some interesting differences. It relates that Chor had four brothers, Sil, Shut, Chetir, and

Mandalash. Because Sil was a troublemaker, always at odds with his brothers, they expelled him from the family home. After wandering in the mountains for some time, Sil finally settled on the east bank of the Panjkora River. When Akund Salak Baba came to Kohistan, he found Sil camped by the riverside. Sil quickly converted to Islam because he hoped to gain an advantage over his brothers by forging an alliance with the saint and his followers. Meanwhile his brothers fled to their fortress cave because they feared strangers. One night Chor dreamt of Mohammed (Peace be upon him*), the last prophet of God. The next day he left the cave, sought out the saint's followers and said to them, "Put me in chains, for I am guilty of sin. I have refused to become a Muslim." The followers of the saint chained his hands and feet, then brought him before the Akund. But the saint said:

"Why have you brought me this man in chains? He is a good man, who has heeded the words of the Holy Prophet (Peace be upon him). Unchain him immediately!"

Chor then said the *Kalima* and became Muslim. Whereupon Akund Salak Baba changed Chor's name to Mir, which means "king." Shut and Chetir followed their brother's example and converted to Islam. Mandalash, on the other hand, refused to accept the one true God and moved to Chitral, where his descendants, later known as the Kalash people, remain Kafirs to this day. A few years later Shut and Mir fought bitterly over conflicting claims to summer pastures, and ended their alliance. Consequently Shut allied with Sil against Mir, and his descendants became a lineage of the Silor clan. Chetir remained an ally of Mir and, accordingly, his descendants became a lineage of the Miror clan.

The inconsistencies in the two versions of the myth are notable, but not because they identify historical inaccuracies. Nor do the consistencies accurately portray historical events. Using either consistencies or inconsistencies to assess historical accuracy is unwise. That Akund Salak Baba is in both versions of the myth does not prove he visited Thull. Nor does it prove he converted Mir and Sil to Islam. It does not even prove that Mir and Sil were real people.

Akund Salak Baba surfaces in the conversion stories of many communities in the Eastern Hindu-Kush region. The people of Thull may have credited him with converting their ancestors because of his reputation as a famous missionary and pious Muslim. His appearance in both versions of the conversion myth may be more related to Thull's claim to status than to historical events. Thull cannot argue that the Holy Prophet converted her ancestors to Islam. Her Pathan neighbors claim this to profess superior status to Kohistanis. At least, however, Akund Salak Baba is an acceptable substitute. Although not as good as the Prophet himself, nevertheless, he validates Thull's claim to equality with neighboring Kohistani communities.

---

*As a sign of deference, Muslims always say "Peace be upon him" whenever they refer to or pronounce the name of Mohammed.

Therefore the significance of the mythic consistencies and inconsistencies lie in what they tell us about Kohistani culture, not what they tell us about Kohistani history. Both consistencies and inconsistencies communicate cultural principles that organize Kohistani social relationships. The myth communicates to—and even instructs—the people of Thull on several levels. We can disentangle the curriculum on the first level into the following strands of meaning:

1. Akund Salak Baba converted the people of Thull to Islam. Therefore they are as good Muslims as the other Kohistani communities converted by the great saint.
2. The Silor claim that they converted to Islam before the Miror and that the Miror renounced paganism only because the Silor left them no alternative. Consequently the Silor are better Muslims and of higher status than the Miror.
3. The Miror admit their ancestor Chor converted to Islam after Sil. Yet, they argue, Sil converted for political gain, whereas Chor converted because he accepted the truth of Islam. Accordingly the Miror are better Muslims and of higher status than the Silor.

At this first level of meaning the myth argues about claims to status. Its discrepancies communicate that neither the Silor nor the Miror acknowledge the other's moral superiority. The outcome of the battle, in other words, is in doubt.

Yet beneath the argument, beneath the discrepancies, lurks agreement. At a deeper level, the argument itself expresses unanimity. Although neither side agrees about who has higher status, nobody disagrees about how to judge status. In other words, at this deeper level the myth isolates cultural principles that structure status hierarchy, namely:

1. Holiness conveys credentials to status.
2. Sincerity of belief positively effects holiness credentials.
3. Given sincerity of belief, the closer in time to the source of holiness, the more impressive the credentials.
4. Holiness credentials (whether of groups or individuals) pass through the male line.

Our understanding of the fight in Kumrat takes on added texture now. The Mulnor (or Mullah Khel) lineage traces descent from a Pathan religious teacher who settled in Thull some generations ago, as you will recall. Even today most of Thull's religious leaders belong to this lineage. Accordingly the Mullah Khel claim more holiness than other lineages because the Holy Prophet himself converted their ancestors to Islam. When the Mullah Khel joined with men from the Silor clan in a feast that explicitly excluded the Miror, the occasion became a statement denigrating the Miror's status as Muslims. That they reacted with violence should surprise no one, because acts that strike at a Muslim's sense of religious worth sometimes lead to such responses, as events like the Salman Rushdie affair so dramatically demonstrate.

Myths about the past communicate contemporary culture, and at the most general level disclose the issues that mobilize kinship groups and define when the segmentary principle affects social relations. At this level myths convey the following message: Segmentary units mobilize to protect their reputation and their rights to natural resources.

And yet clans and lineages no longer control natural resources within Thull and therefore no longer fight over pastures because a lottery annually redistributes grazing rights. In contrast, lineages in the neighboring Kohistani communities of Kalkot and Kinorlam still own permanent rights to summer pastures, and disputes over grazing rights can lead to fighting in which men lose their lives.

Thus segmentary opposition operates disjointedly in Thull. It is especially relevant at the level of the community. Thull's citizens believe their neighbors to be rapacious, that they will steal their forests and pastures at any opportunity. Consequently they are always prepared to put aside internal disputes and unite as a *qaom* to meet outside threats with deadly force. Clans and lineages—the constituent units of the *qaom*—do not view one another with such suspicion, because descent groups cannot fight over the scarce natural resources they do not own. On the rare occasions men from other *dum*s publicly denigrate a descent group's status, its members unite to oppose their detractors. But words, rather than physical force, most often provide the form such opposition takes, although these disputes can always escalate to violence, as the events in Kumrat confirm.

Segmentary opposition is, however, relevant in one other context. The Pakistani government created a series of district councils throughout rural Pakistan. These councils were (and continue to be) composed of members from local communities chosen by election. The council is headed by a "chair," also elected by members of local communities in the district. The main function of councils and their "chairmen" is to assist in implementing government policy; they have little power either to change or formulate policy on their own.

Nevertheless Kohistanis value seats on their district council because it sometimes allocates funds for minor development projects. For example, a sports club founded by members of the emerging professional elite in Dir town received money to asphalt its basketball court from the District Council of northern Dir. (I refer those interested in the sports club and basketball in Dir to my article, "Rim Shots and Rifle Fire" in the September 1986 issue of *Natural History.*) More importantly, though, holding seats on the district council provides politicians with an opportunity to forge personal relationships with local and even national government officials. In a country where administrators often make economic decisions on the basis of personal relationships, membership on district councils can lead to economic success.

The 1983 race for a council seat in Thull pitted the two biggest timber contractors in the community against one another in a fiercely contested election. Dilaram Sher belonged to the Silor clan, whereas Ahmad Shah came from the Meskol clan. Both appealed to segmentary values in soliciting votes from fellow clan members—and naturally so, according to men in

Thull. If, for instance, opposing candidates were from different lineages of the same clan, they said, their lineages would support them. If they were from different clans, their clans would support them. And if they were from different communities, their community would support them. The world worked that way.

But the world does not always work that way in Thull. Segmentary opposition is only one consideration among several affecting how men vote for district council members. The structure of kinship networks, the second dimension of Kohistani kinship, affects voting as much as mindless segmentary loyalties.

Segmentary opposition, however, does provide Kohistanis with a bare-bones framework for understanding election politics. Although it may not mechanically produce voting blocs, it has more subtle consequences. Candidates realize they cannot automatically depend on political support from their lineage or clan because of the segmentary rule alone. Yet at the same time, they believe other descent groups will vote for their members, more often than not. That perception affects how candidates formulate election strategies.

The segmentary rule, therefore, works fitfully and sporadically; it has different significance at different levels of segmentation. It rarely determines how people act in any automatic fashion. Yet even when it does not mechanically produce political alliances, segmentary opposition helps organize people's perceptions of the world, perceptions which affect how they weigh the strategic value of their choices.

KINSHIP NETWORKS

Thinking about kinship as groups leads us to consider Thull social organization from the top down, as a two-dimensional triangle. We begin with the community at the triangle's apex, then move down, first to the community's constituent clans and finally to the clans' constituent lineages. But kinship in Thull has a second dimension, which also frames political maneuver. We must switch our vantage point to understand this dimension, focusing on individuals rather than groups. Kinship looks like overlapping networks, which can be understood from this perspective by looking from the center to the periphery.

Every individual in Thull stands at the center of a kinship universe built from relationships of four kinds, namely, *babatani, dadatani, momotani,* and *isotani.* The first two, *babatani* and *dadatani,* form concentric circles of agnation (agnates are those people tracing kinship relationships through male links only). Although *baba* is the Kohistani word for "father," and *dada* the word for "grandfather," Kohistanis use the terms metaphorically to distinguish close from distant agnates in this context. *Babatani* usually include people linked by a common grandfather, but when the pool of close agnates is small, people enlarge their *babatani* network to include more distant agnates as well. *Dadatani,* in contrast, are usually those kin belonging to one's *lukut dum.*

Because *dadatani* and *lukut dum* sometimes include the same people, one might think *dadatani* (and by extension *babatani*) are units in the segmentary lineage system. That would be a mistake. They comprise sections of ego-centered kinship networks ordered from center to periphery, rather than groups with distinct boundaries arranged in a hierarchical structure from top to bottom. Accordingly, agnatic kinship networks sometimes overlap. Lineages, by comparison, have distinct boundaries that unambiguously include some while excluding others.

Momotani and *isotani* notions play with agnation in a different way. Both categories consist of agnates, but unlike *babatani* the linking person is female. Specifically *momotani* are one's mother's *babatani,* while *isotani* are one's wife's *babatani.*

Kohistanis draw from the various sections of their kinship network for political and economic support. They believe a person's *babatani, isotani,* and *momotani* will naturally help in whatever way they can whenever the need arises. If a man requires assistance in repairing his house, for example, kin from these categories will aid him; if his enemies threaten him, the same people will champion his cause. By comparison, *dadatani* have less obligation to provide active support, although people believe their *dadatani* will favor them even if the support is "silent" (that is, covert). *Dadatani* can become one's deadly enemies, though, as Qai Afsal's *dushmani* demonstrated. Yet Kohistanis believe that enmity between *dadatani* demonstrates a failure of character. It rarely occurs, they say, and rightfully so. Qai Afsal, interestingly enough, denies his enemy Khan Akbar is *dadatani,* as others assert, even though Khan Akbar is a member of the same *lukut dum,* the Hasanor. Qai Afsal insists his *dadatani* include only those descended from Malik Pir, while within that category his *babatani* contain only brothers and paternal first cousins (see Figure 8).

Focusing on descent as a hierarchical structure, and kin relationships as structures of individual-centered networks, helps us understand something about the connection between politics and kinship in Thull. Yet thinking about kinship only as consistent patterns veils as well as illuminates. Kinship structures in Thull include inconsistencies and ambiguities which strain the neatness of their organizational configurations. By their nature these inconsistencies and ambiguities unfold options, establish possibilities for negotiation, and create opportunities to exploit weaknesses and strengths. Qai Afsal's enemies maligned his character by using kinship against him. He responded by using ambiguities inherent in the system to defend himself.

Even the ambiguities and inconsistencies are not written in stone, however. Kinship is as much a process as a structure, so the interconnection of kinship and politics is itself a process. The relationship between marriage and kinship networks furnishes a case in point. Kohistanis are centered in networks made from four categories of kin. These will overlap (that is, one person's *babatani* will be another's *isotani,* for example) if people marry

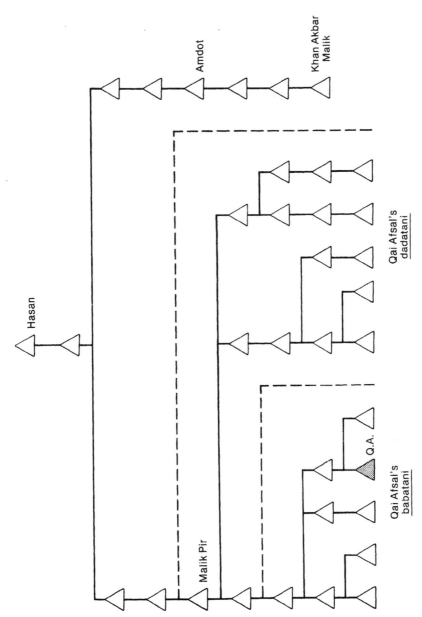

Figure 8   Partial Genealogy of Qai Afsal's Male Agnates

outside their *lukut dum* ("lineage"). Lineage exogamy (marrying outside one's lineage) also assures that each kinship category will include sets of different people.

These structural properties of networks can affect politics in several ways. First, overlapping networks create conflicting allegiances that inhibit political conflicts, as shown with *lud* in an earlier chapter. Second, lineage exogamy makes the choice of marriage partner politically strategic, since marriage forms alliances between distinct groups of agnates. Who one marries determines one's own *isotani* allies, for example, and the *momotani* allies of one's children.

Marriage does not mechanically follow rules of lineage exogamy, however. Even though most marriages do connect people from different lineages (and to a lesser extent different clans, according to census information), I also discovered marriages linking *dadatani,* and even *babatani.* Everyone I asked, interestingly enough, insisted that the people of Thull always marry *babatani* unless no one from that category is available. Specifically people claimed a strong preference for marriage with paternal cousins.

Thus marriage patterns in Thull fluctuate. Sometimes marriage links agnates, at other times groups of agnates. Lineage endogamy and exogamy shift in Thull, and the shifting pattern produces rippling kinship networks. When marriages connect agnatic kin, *babatani, isotani,* and *momotani* categories coalesce. Paternal cousin marriage, for example, produces fathers-in-law (*isotani*), who are the same people as fathers' brothers (*babatani*) (see Figure 9). When marriages break the preference rule for paternal cousins, kinship categories separate. Consequently the web of kinship in Thull shifts as paternal cousin marriage isolates some sections and marriages outside lineages expand, reconnect, and overlap other sections. These constant changes in the kinship context affect political processes. The force of conflicting allegiances waxes and wanes, for example, and the significance of marriage in forging political alliances wavers.

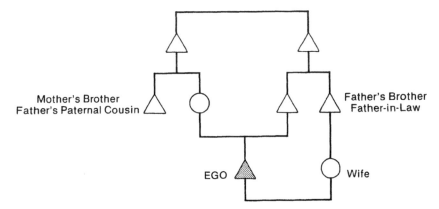

Figure 9   Paternal Cousin Marriage

7 / The Contortion
of Politics

Politics is getting the other guy before he gets you.

I forgot who said this—perhaps a big city mayor somewhere, or an obscure Pentagon general, or a Mississippi Sheriff, or even Al Capone. In any case, thinking about politics as a struggle between rivals for control over people and resources, a competitive contest resembling a complex game of "king-of-the-mountain," proves a useful and interesting way of looking at politics in many societies. Fredrik Barth proposed it to anthropology in a book about politics in Swat, the valley adjacent to Dir in the east. His study of political leadership among Yusufzai Pathans, published in 1959, remains an anthropological classic even today.

Barth assumes that strategy, more than moral rules, determines how people act. For example, we learn among the Yusufzai of Swat that ambitious men shed old allies and take on new ones to advance their interests and defeat rivals. In the process they create patterns in the political minuet. Our earlier study of death enmity showed that moral values twist behavior as much as the passion for personal advantage. Even so, emphasizing the motivational power of self-interest in politics reveals that when opposed political aims dominate relationships, they often inspire the choices people make.

The political dance does not take place in a vacuum, however; cultural values and configurations of social organization form contexts that affect its pattern. Moreover the contexts which mold patterns of political competition are not immutable. We must study carefully those confluences in time when new ideas undermine the common understandings upholding systems of power, authority, and legitimacy. When cultural values clash and people hold conflicting visions of the human condition, recurring patterns of political competition often disintegrate. From the disorder people construct new configurations of values and new forms of political organization. Yet before the new order establishes itself, sociocultural organization becomes a process of change.

Thull is at one of these critical junctures in time. Shared understandings and political forms are changing. Now people in Thull fashion, challenge, revise, and challenge again, basic values, cultural definitions of reality, and rules of behavior. Death enmity lies at the center of this process.

THE POLITICAL CONSEQUENCES OF DUSHMANI

In the last chapter I mentioned some of the consequences of death enmity for Thull social organization. We saw there that *dushmani* weighs ego-centered kinship networks in favor of descent groups. In this chapter we will study these changes in more detail by focusing on the relationship between death enmity and political organization. My starting point will be Kohistani political organization as described by Fredrik Barth some thirty years ago.

Barth found in 1954 that Kohistanis did not distinguish political factions from lineages. Unlike their Pathan neighbors to the south, descent usually determined both alliances and oppositions. Lineages also operated as economic units, and their economic strength ultimately determined their political power.

Kohistani communities generally solved internal conflicts in village councils (*jirgas*); they formed the most important context for political competition. Barth describes the organization of councils as follows:

> The council members (*ghyan*) each represent an "extended family"—i.e. a group larger than the household but smaller than the major subsections of the community. A council member will thus speak for himself and his brothers, brother's sons, his paternal cousins, and their sons, and rarely for a wider group than that. . . . Only owners of land are qualified to sit in the council, and the ability to speak and argue a case well is emphasized.
>
> In the council, members sit randomly mixed, and there is no ranking of seats—all present are regarded as equals in their capacity as council members. There is no notion that the representatives of one section [that is, lineage] should sit together. . . . [O]n the contrary, their corporative capacity as a body representing the *village* as a homogenous unit is emphasized in the mixing and equality of the council members. (1956:63)

Although descent groups were not formally recognized in *jirgas*, they nevertheless played an important role in council politics for strategic reasons. When the council brought men before it for committing a serious wrong, it treated their acts as wrongs against the community. Formally, men participated in council affairs as members of their community, rather than lineage representatives. Yet each man's political strength depended on the economic strength of his lineage, and that depended in large part on the lineage's size. Consequently, skillful politics in councils meant maneuvering mild punishments for the members of one's own descent group whenever possible, so that the culprit would not be lost to the lineage. Once penalties were set, senior politicians often helped their junior lineage mates fulfill the conditions of punishment to maintain the strength of the group. Hence, according to Barth:

> in the solution of conflicts, the segmentary system of sections (lineages) does not operate, as a lineage system would, through the oppositions of segments—there is a definite conception of the village council as a body, responsible for the maintenance of law and order. But in the execution of the verdicts reached by

this council, the sectional (descent) hierarchy is mobilized, by virtue of the strategic implications following from their constitution as "political parties." (1956:65)

The value of preserving village peace through the maintenance of law and order also affected Kohistani politics by providing cultural rationales for council decisions. Thus Kohistanis thought of murder, adultery, and theft as offenses against the community punishable (in theory, at least) by death or exile, so that troublemakers would be removed from the community, and law and order maintained.

In Thull death enmity changed this pattern of political organization by changing the sociocultural context for political maneuver. *Dushmani* involved new ideas about murder and adultery. It questioned the idea that such misdeeds were primarily crimes against the community, defining them more as violations of a personal integrity given men by God. Consequently men understood them as potential assaults on their identity as Muslims. Murder and adultery became entrapped in what is called the greater *jihad,* which binds together the interrelated themes of struggle, death, and paradise fundamental to Islam.

JIHAD

Jihad is widely misunderstood in the West. It conjures up visions of wild-eyed, sword-wielding fanatics hell-bent on slaughtering infidels in a holy war (Shahrani and Canfield 1984:27,225), a misconception emerging from the early confrontation in the Old World between the forces of Christianity and Islam. Like many of our popular notions of non-Western cultures, it is fundamentally flawed.

Jihad is a notion rich with myriad shades of meaning. For a deeper discussion of its complexities than will be attempted here I refer those interested to Shahrani's Introduction to *Revolutions and Rebellions in Afghanistan* (1984) and Metcalf's "Islamic Reform and Islamic Women" in *Moral Conduct and Authority* (1984). Both are excellent sources with detailed bibliographies.

Jihad is the battle against evil all Muslims must undertake if they are to reach paradise after death. This struggle takes two general forms: the lesser and greater *jihad.* The lesser *jihad* is the armed struggle against non-Muslim political powers who threaten Islam with physical force, while the greater *jihad* is the personal struggle against the evil lurking within everyone.

Agreements about what constitutes *jihad* are obviously an important part of the cultural context organizing politics in Thull. But these common understandings are no longer as common as they once were—especially those understandings about what constitutes the greater *jihad.* Hence people often quarrel about courses of action. Are they "Kafir work" (and hence manifestations of evil), or "Mussalman work" (behavior willed by God)? Are they temptations to be withstood in the struggle against evil, or are they permitted—even required—behavior according to the tenets of Islam? Thull is at a point in its history when often no clear answers exist.

For example, the Koran demands an eye for an eye, and some Kohistanis think of vengeance in terms of the greater *jihad*. It is part of the struggle to walk in God's path, to lead the life of the exemplary Muslim. Yet others argue that the good Muslim must nurture the community's well-being, even it if means foregoing revenge.

Thus the values of vengeance and community peace clash with no clear winner emerging. Should a good Muslim, one engaged in the internal struggle with evil, seek village peace, or cleanse his *ghrairat,* his gift from God, by taking vengeance? Kohistani culture provides only ambiguous answers now. Consequently people often resist settling murder and adultery cases in councils, preferring to seek personal revenge instead. Many cases never end in settlements, and those that do are often preceded by violent confrontations.

In such confrontations men mobilize personal networks rather than lineages, both in seeking vengeance and in protecting against it. Moreover, as *dushmani* increased in importance, political networks became critical in other contexts as well. Alternatively the significance of lineages withered in politics. Kohistanis borrowed *dala* (the Pushto word meaning "political faction"), to refer to such networks, and *dalabasi* (roughly, the confrontation between *dala*s) became the Kohistani word for politics. The distinction between descent and political action groups now is as important among Kohistanis as it is among Pakhtuns.

POLITICAL NETWORKS

Men construct *dala* networks from various categories of social relationships. These networks always include kinship categories but are not limited to kinship. Thus *babatani* (close agnates) and *momotani* (mother's *babatani*) always belong to one's *dala. Isotani* (wife's *babatani*) and *dadatani* (distant agnates) are more often "silent" *dala* members, since their support is usually covert. "Silent" members do not participate in fighting and do not mobilize when *dala*s confront one another. If, however, a person from the *isotani* or *babatani* category activates *dala* membership by actually participating in fights with his relative's enemies, the men who stand in the same relationship to the enemy must also activate their membership in the opposing *dala*s. For example, if a man's brothers-in-law fight at his side, his enemy's brothers-in-law must also join the fighting.

This has consequences for strategic maneuver. Mir Said, married to Qai Afsal's sister, never participated in the gunfights between Qai Afsal and Khan Akbar because Khan Akbar had many brothers-in-law. If Mir Said had fought on Qai Afsal's behalf, then all of Khan Akbar's brothers-in-law would have fought on the opposing side, thus increasing Khan Akbar's strength relative to Qai Afsal.

Dosotani

Yet no one can predict the actions of a silent *dala* member, and in the heat of any moment he might kill his ally's enemy if the opportunity presents itself. Alam, a silent member of Gul Mir's *dala,* tried to kill Gutkar Khan because he insulted Gul Mir, calling him a barking dog. Alam aimed his AK-47 at Gutkar Khan, but bystanders threw themselves between the two men before Alam could fire his machine gun, thereby saving Gutkar Khan's life.

Still, most "silent" *dala* members keep their participation covert, which usually means limiting their activities to gathering and passing intelligence. "Silent" members disclose whatever they discover about their ally's enemy. Information about an enemy's whereabouts, for instance, can be crucial, both in devising successful schemes to kill him, or, alternatively, in avoiding his vengeance. Consequently the number of a man's "silent" allies significantly influences his political effectiveness.

Men also build *dalas* from the *dosotani* category of relationship. *Dosotani* generally means "relations of friendship." This category is especially important in determining political strength for two reasons. First, its composition can fluctuate. Birth determines one's *babatani* and *momotani;* therefore men can do nothing to change the size of these categories. In contrast, men create *dosotani* by their own actions. Moreover, when kinsmen quarrel they still remain kin, but when friends quarrel the relationship may not survive. Consequently, individuals burdened with deadly enemies must carefully cultivate friendships in order to maintain or increase their political strength. Second, *dosotani* increases the number of "silent" *dala* members. If a man belongs to a *dala* because of friendship, then his close kin, both *babatani* and *momotani,* will favor that *dala,* becoming silent members. And a man can always call on his friend's kinsmen for more active help if their counterparts in the opposing *dala* act against him.

Finally, *dalas* include men who belong purely for political expediency. I could find no Kohistani word for this category of political ally. But my friends all agreed that such members are distinctive, since no moral dimension potentiates their obligations to the *dala.* Their dependability is always suspect and often short-lived, for they can easily switch loyalties. Such men are only peripheral allies, constituting the smallest number of a man's supporters. Nevertheless they can provide the measure of victory in any given fight.

DISPUTES

Opposition between *dalas* manifests itself in disputes between individuals and their allies, called in Kohistani *jars.* Kohistanis distinguish among *jars* (as they do among lineages) in terms of their size. *Gin jars* are disputes involving large numbers of allies, whereas *likit jars* involve only a few participants. Men call a dispute *jar* whether it evokes physical violence or only an exchange of verbal insults. Kohistanis make these distinctions by describing what actually happened. If the *jar* were verbal, for example, people would say literally, "They made noise"; if it involved an exchange of gunfire, "They gave one another rifles."

Jars begin whenever two people argue. Often an uninvolved third person assumes the role of mediator and convinces the disputants to settle their argument peacefully. If he fails, word spreads that fighting is imminent, and *dalas* mobilize against one another.

Many issues initiate *jars*. Disagreements over ownership of property, accusations of theft, shoveling snow from one's own roof onto neighbors' roofs, grazing animals in other groups' summer pastures, killing and eating other men's animals, and staring at women are some of the more common causes of disputes. Disagreements over property, like accusations of staring at women, are the most difficult to settle immediately and, therefore, most often result in confrontations between *dalas*.

Disputes often begin when men claim (*lanja*) the property of others. If, for instance, a man accuses another of stealing a cow, he will claim compensation for the theft. Alternatively a dispute may start when someone claims that a particular field or house owned by another man actually belongs to him.

Claiming land and houses is endemic in Thull politics because rules of ownership sometimes lead to ambiguous title. Men own both houses and fields individually. Such property can be bought and sold within the community, although outsiders cannot buy immovable property.

Men usually gain land by inheriting rather than buying it. Both brothers and sisters are entitled to share their father's property in accordance with Muslim law, although sons qualify for shares twice as large as those of their sisters. Few, if any, women, however, actually possess land as part of their inheritance. All animals, houses, and guns are inherited by sons.

Brothers share equally in their father's estate, but the property is divided at different times. Each brother acquires most of his inheritance upon marriage, before his father's death. Brothers usually marry in the order of their birth. Consequently a father parcels his estate piecemeal to his sons over a period of some years, always keeping a portion for himself. Yet he does not remain economically inactive, and thus the size of the portion he retains sometimes increases and decreases during these years. If his resources have dwindled when his youngest son marries, for example, then his elder sons should contribute to their younger brother's share. But they may be hard-pressed themselves, and promise to contribute at a later time instead. Whether they keep the promise is an open question.

These inheritance rules often create conflicting claims on land, usually among the descendants of brothers. Yet men rarely claim land from their relatives. That would damage the relationship, weakening their political power in the process. When a man sells land, however, he loses interest in it, which, in turn, creates an opportunity for his kinsmen to claim it. After the sale they can assert their claims without harming relationships with him.

Sometimes men claim land long after it has been sold. In fact, the more time elapses, the easier it is to claim it, because people often forget the details of past land ownership. A man can claim land by asserting that his grandmother was wrongfully denied her inheritance, for example. Alternatively he can claim a particular field by maintaining that it really belonged to his grandfather rather than to his grandfather's brother, who sold it in years past. And, of course, men can always argue that land lost by an ancestor in a past land dispute was claimed unjustly, and claim it back.

Title to land is further obscured by the absence of a system of land recording or registration. Therefore most men can manufacture some kind of claim on the land of another if they choose. Although no exact figures exist, my friends maintained that powerful men in Thull often pursue such claims, and consequently much land changes ownership through what is little more than theft. In the final analysis, therefore, many land titles are only as good as the firepower that backs them.

Recently government officials attempted to institute land registration in Thull but met with little cooperation. Most people agree it would only make a bad situation worse. Poor men fear that those with wealth and education would enjoy a greater opportunity to steal their land. Rich men could challenge the registration and win the land by bribing government officials and manipulating court processes. Powerful men fear that government officials would gain power over them if a system of recorded deeds existed. For then the officials would know exactly who owned which fields, a knowledge that would enable them to extract bribes by threatening to confiscate the land. So land remains unrecorded, titles remain questionable, and *dalabasi* flourishes.

Disputes of all kinds (but land disputes in particular) often result in clashes between opposed *dala*. If death results, *dushmani* begins, and the dispute becomes difficult to end. Often, however, no one dies, even though adversaries exchange blows and even bullets. If no winner emerges after a number of such encounters, the protagonists usually agree to settle the dispute in a council, or *jirga*.

COUNCILS

Dala politics and *dushmani* have made the council system in Thull more complex than the earlier system described by Barth. Now councils are convened for many reasons—sometimes to make policy decisions, sometimes to resolve land disputes, sometimes to end *dushmani,* and sometimes to punish wrongdoers. The size of councils and their composition varies with the particular case. If the case is a dispute—between brothers, for example—then the *jirga* convened to settle it will be composed of elder brothers, or paternal cousins if no elder brothers exist. If the dispute is between unrelated men, the council will include men not in the *dala* of either disputant. Thus a rough segmentary principal operates in the compositions of dispute *jirga*s. The closer the relationship between the disputants, the closer the relationship between the disputants and the mediators. Thus brothers mediate between brothers, cousins between cousins, neighbors between neighbors.

Jirga *debate*

Men in the community also convene *jirga*s to deal with specific problems. For instance, the teachers at the primary school in Thull convened a *jirga* when the school watchman came to work armed with an AK-47 because he feared his death enemies. Not surprisingly, the threat of a gun battle at the school disrupted classes, which created an intolerable situation for the teachers. Members of this *jirga* were chosen by the teachers from the pool of noted mediators in the community, with the exception of those in the *dala*s of both the watchman and his enemies.

Councils also meet to punish those who commit "crimes" against the community. An act is "criminal" in the Kohistani sense if it can be punished by a fine (*jaram*). For instance, if a man allows his animals to graze in another *lud*'s pasture area, if he keeps his animals in the core settlement too long in the spring, if he brings them into the core settlement too soon in the fall, if he cuts branches for animal fodder before the permitted time, if he fails to clean and repair the main irrigation channels that water his fields, community *jirga*s can fine him. These are the kind of councils described by Barth in 1954. They are comprised of all male households heads from the community, as they were thirty years ago.

The councils are different, however, in one important respect. Because death enmity became so important in community affairs, the groups concerned with their political strength in council politics are now *dala* rather than lineages. As a result, when men cannot pay fines, relatives from all kinship categories contribute toward paying them, not just members of their lineages.

*Jirga*s meeting to dispense fines gather in a central place, often on the large rooftop known as *torwaloshan,* or in the area of spring pastures called Kumrat if the weather is good. Other councils have no specific meeting place. Usually councils convene to settle disputes gather after noon prayer, when all its members are present.

After the *jirga* decides an equitable settlement, the entire group visits each disputant, urging him to accept their verdict. If either man refuses, then more men join the council, adding their weight to the voices of the other members. Increasing the council's size often convinces men to accept its decision, since they must provide hospitality for the entire council during its visit.

The disputants themselves, or else heads of households, choose the members of most *jirgas,* although household heads comprise the councils convened to dispense fines. The men of Thull choose council members on the basis of their reputation. Some men are known to be convincing orators, for example. Others are thought to be particularly wise, and others possess special knowledge.

Theft cases offer a particularly interesting example of how such councils work. A man whose property is stolen first hires someone he trusts to find the thief. If the investigator is successful and the thief unmasked, the case goes before a *jirga* composed of members chosen by both the victim and the alleged thief from a pool of men known in Thull to be wise and just. If the evidence is convincing, damages are awarded based on the value of the stolen items and the cost of hiring the investigator.

Both parties usually accept the *jirga*'s judgment, for if either refuses, the case goes to a government court, an outcome that is against everyone's interest. Government courts usually find the accused guilty and levy heavier fines than village *jirga*s. Consequently, accepting the verdict of the *jirga* is always in the best interest of those accused of theft. Accepting the *jirga*'s verdict is also in the best interest of theft victims, for members of government courts "eat" fines themselves and give victims nothing.

POLITICAL LEADERSHIP

Death enmity affected religious and secular leaders in Thull by influencing the distribution of political power and authority between them. Religious leaders throughout the Northwest Frontier seem an odd species to outside observers. Often they are powerless—even the object of scorn and ridicule. Many of my friends mercilessly derided one particular religious figure from the area, calling him "cow mullah" because of his alleged stupidity and rather substantial girth. Yet at other times these same people wield immense power, becoming the rallying point for political movements encompassing communities and even entire areas.

In Thull *jihad,* the struggle against evil, determines when religious leaders are politically preeminent. They rally armed opposition against non-Muslims who threaten Islam, and they determine the rules of behavior necessary to battle the evil within everyone. If the community agrees a matter concerns *jihad,* then religious leaders can, and indeed must, wield political authority.

Agreements about what constitutes *jihad* are obviously an important part of the cultural context organizing politics in Thull. Today religious leaders strive to expand its scope, thus increasing their political power. Their main resource is the authority to interpret the wellsprings of absolute truth—the Koran (the word of God) and the Hidith (the sayings of the Holy Prophet). Still, secular leaders resist surrendering long-held beliefs, especially when it shrinks their political influence. Consequently, common understandings about the limits of the greater *jihad* are no longer as common as they once were, and people quarrel about courses of action.

This has obvious implications for the opposition between revenge and village peace, as I discussed earlier. Should men categorically pursue revenge in their personal struggle against evil, or does Islam permit (and even require) men to sacrifice vengeance if it promotes communal harmony? Thull is at a point in its history when often no unambiguous answer exists.

We should not be surprised, therefore, that religious leaders rarely preach against *dushmani.* When men insist on taking the Koranic "eye for an eye" in lieu of settling death enmity in councils, it reduces the political effectiveness of secular leaders. At the same time, it expands the scope of the greater *jihad,* thus bolstering the authority of religious leaders.

Secular leaders—those most often chosen to serve on councils—are called *maliks.* The word means "chief" or "headman" in Pushto, but is better understood as "leader/elder" in Kohistani. Sometimes people use *malik* as a term of respect for elderly men. And sometimes it is simply a part of a man's name, having no political significance. In political contexts, however, *malik* refers to the men of importance in the community.

No permanent *malik* position exists to which people can be elected or which they can inherit. Leadership in Thull is less fixed than this. Men become *maliks* slowly, over a period of many years. If they demonstrate wisdom and skill at arbitrating disputes and if they use their skills to help others (relatives, friends, community members), they will gradually become *maliks,* respected and followed by others. Wealth, piety, and a large number of close male relatives provide added advantages.

Because of *dushmani,* the political influence of *maliks* today depends more on the strength of their political network or party than their lineage. However, even though lineages are no longer the most important source of a *malik*'s power, they are still significant in some situations. When a problem arises affecting the entire community, the men of importance in Thull call a council of household heads to discuss it. *Maliks* known as good orators speak to clarify the issue and initiate discussions of ways the problem might be solved. After the general opinion of the council is clear, the men present chose *maliks* to serve on a smaller council charged with solving the problem. To make these councils representative of everyone in the community,

Maliks *of Thull*

the *jirga* chooses one *malik* from each minor lineage. These smaller councils sometimes meet with counterpart *jirgas* from other communities, either to settle disputes or coordinate common political action. In 1984 a council convened to mediate the *dushmani* between Wali Khan of Thull and Safar Maluk of Kalkot. A few years earlier, councils from all the Kohistani communities in Dir organized a march on the government post in the town of Shiringal to protest the government's timber policy.

Even here, though, violence made itself evident. When word spread that a contingent of government soldiers opened fire on the marchers, a series of violent confrontations between government forces and local people exploded in several locations. Government officials isolated the entire district by cutting all roads, and called in troops armed with heavy weapons (artillery, tanks, and fighter bombers). Kohistanis organized their men to fight using an organizational model borrowed from the Tablighi Jamma'at, described in Chapter 3. Warfare ended when government negotiators agreed to increase timber royalties.

This particular incident, as much as any other, demonstrates the new political reality in which Kohistanis must operate. Events and forces outside Kohistan now, more than ever, create problems that Kohistanis must solve, often in novel ways. As a result, Kohistani political organization is fluid, its structure changing.

Death enmity affected Thull politics in several ways: It strengthened the political significance of political networks while weakening descent groups; it increased the complexity of the council system; and it disorganized the distribution of power and authority between religious and secular leaders. *Dushmani* situated Kohistanis within "Kalashnikov Culture," as some call the Pakhtun tribal areas of the Northwest Frontier, where the AK-47 symbolizes the violent quality of male social relations. Consequently Kohistani political organization resembles Pathan politics more closely now than it did before. As my landlord remarked, "We may be Kohistanis, but we consider ourselves Pakhtun."

8 / The Politics
of Fieldwork

Shahid was discouraged. "The people of Thull," he said, "are very harsh." Shahid had just returned from five o'clock prayer. Once again during the discussion that always followed the actual prayer, someone had criticized him for working with me. "Good Muslims should have nothing to do with Kafirs!" the man had said. "Working for Kafirs is a sin because they teach you immoral behavior." For about an hour the argument raged, both sides quoting from the Koran and the Hadith to support their positions. Although Shahid had the more sophisticated command of Islamic law (his grandfather was a noted Muslim cleric), he was unable to convince his detractors.

Throughout my stay in Thull, many people remained convinced I was a creature sent by the devil to harm the community. The stories of my alleged evil doings always amazed me, both in their number and detail. One was a particular favorite. According to this story, I asked questions about history to steal the forests of Thull. Men swore they saw me burying forged historical documents that would prove my ancestors owned the forests. Obviously, they said, I planned to return some years hence, "discover" the forged documents, and claim all timber royalties for myself.

Shahid and I often discussed how best to counter the rumors about me and concluded that doing fieldwork in Thull was a test of our political guile. It was a test I failed, for a *jirga* of my most vocal opponents ultimately forced me to leave Thull three months before I had planned.

Being asked to leave a community is a failure anthropologists find especially difficult to accept. We like to think we forge close personal ties with the people we study and, indeed, often base the authority of our ethnographic analysis on having created just such close relationships. Obviously, I have difficulty claiming the people of Thull as "my people" because so many of them never ceased to despise me. Consequently I can't claim authority based on "being a member of the tribe."

Still, I learned from being hated, and I learned from the events surrounding my leaving Thull. These experiences, however, cast my account in certain shades and hues. They affected the angle from which I observed Thull and influenced my understanding of what I saw.

That doesn't mean this book is only a figment of my imagination. I observed real events; people acted toward me in real ways. But much of my understanding came from navigating through peculiar experiences. Consequently the reader should know something of that journey to put my ethnography in perspective. What follows, then, is a record of field research based mostly on my personal journal. I have not included everything in the journal; some entries were too rambling to be relevant, and some too personal to be shared. What I have attempted to include is the events (and my reactions to them) that particularly affected my understanding of Thull.

April 3

We finally arrived in Thull! I thought I would go crazy in the preceding weeks waiting, waiting, waiting. But, at the same time, I began the trip with a slight sense of foreboding. The people here seem so much harder, if not crueler, than the Sum (the Kohistanis in Afghanistan I had worked with in the 1960s). Possibly it's a stronger Pakhtun influence. As our landlord said, "We may be Kohistanis, but we consider ourselves Pakhtun."

Our landlord told us we should not talk to anyone but him. All other men were bad. But he looks like a mafioso hit man to me. I'm in bad trouble if I can only talk to him. And, he said, we should never leave our yard. How can I do fieldwork like that!?

The police came later this evening—the head constable and two of his men. The head constable told us about some Europeans who hiked over the mountains to Thull a few years ago. They stayed in what is now the police post—then a "rest house." At night they were robbed and I think sodomized, but Shahid seemed reluctant to translate that part.

Gul Shah came after the police left. He told us that those particular Europeans had neither the government's nor the community's permission to be here. Because a *jirga* gave us permission to live in Thull, we have nothing to fear. But we should be careful of bad people. (The police said we shouldn't trust anyone—they were all bad—and we should never meet anyone at night.) Most of the people in Thull are honorable, Gul Shah said, but some are not. He will tell us who the bad people are. We should not let these people into our house, but outside we can meet and talk to anyone.

Certainly at least some people seemed friendly when we came. We had no trouble getting our possessions carried to the house and we had a shit-load! Dilaram Sher's son, among others, helped us. Later Dilaram Sher himself came to pay his respects—his pistol prominently displayed. His son accompanied him, armed with a machine gun.

April 15

Today was quite a day. In the morning I spent a lot of time with a man called Anwar, learning Kohistani. I think I finally found a good language teacher. In the afternoon a horde of people descended on our house for medicine. Three of them were especially notorious gunmen, I later learned. This created a big fuss with our neighbors. They didn't want these particular

My house in Thull

people anywhere close to their house. Then there was an incident with our washing water. Abida (Shahid's wife) threw it over the side of our roof—unfortunately, onto the heads of some people below. The incident drew a crowd of about sixty angry men. Dilaram Sher made peace, but suggested afterwards a better place for us to live.

When I saw the other house I knew we should move. We would rent the upper part. It includes two bedrooms, a kitchen, two bathrooms, and a latrine. The owners, three brothers, live with their families below. The house also has room for my jeep.

April 16

Today we moved. This house is much better. I spent a lot of time with Anwar. He told Shahid that he didn't like me because I am a Kafir, but Shahid shamed him by pointing out the hospitality he took from me. Regardless of his personal feelings, he is a good informant. I have to accept that it doesn't matter what people think of me as long as I can work. I'm here to do research, not to win popularity contests. Still it's difficult to be the person everyone despises, especially because I'm not used to it.

May 4

This was a significant day . . . well, significant in what happened and my reactions to it. Today was the first time in my life I saw serious injuries.

The children of the house

A man and two boys were injured by a blast of dynamite set off at a wedding. The man had internal injuries. He was spitting blood, had cuts on his chest, legs, and feet, and his hand was mangled beyond belief! His fingers were almost torn from his hand. They were twisted into grotesque shapes with bones and knuckle joints showing. It reminded me of a turkey leg torn from the turkey at Thanksgiving. Most Americans are protected from this kind of violent injury. Coming face to face with it almost made me sick.

May 14

Today I was feeling particularly down. I really miss Lael (my daughter who at the time was a junior in high school), especially when I have no contact through the mail. I don't know what she's doing, how she is. I wonder if all this is really worth it. I'm giving away these last years with her, and I wonder if the price is too high.

May 15

We walked to Golam Sarwar's house in the mountains for lunch. He served a real feast—bread, chicken, eggs, and spinach. I gathered some interesting information on history from Golam Sarwar's father and on *dushmani* from the other men present. About fifteen men were there, all armed with rifles of various kinds. I've rarely seen any man in Thull who wasn't armed with some kind of weapon. After I returned home, Gul Shah stopped for a visit and told me about Kohistani military organization.

Today was a good day. I learned a lot.

May 16

I spent most of the day writing my notes from yesterday, but did work with Anwar on language. Kohistani is difficult for me to learn. I often have feelings of hopelessness these days. Everything I learn suggests endless series of new questions. Sociocultural systems are so complex; I don't think I will ever understand this one.

May 19

For some reason I am more homesick than usual tonight. I listened to the tape of our supper club in Middletown. That world seems so far away. The tape made me see things about my life at home that I usually accept without thinking . . . and, which I sorely miss—men and women sharing a meal and discussing a film, for example. My friends at home eat together once a week and never realize that what they do is not only impossible but unthinkable here.

May 20

I learned from Gul Shah that a number of men are opposed to my living in Thull. During a meeting of maliks at the school, a man called Sharazam came to argue against me. He is a member of a group called the Tablighi Jamma'at. It is some kind of pan Islamic brotherhood of preachers. He told the maliks gathered at the school that I have a secret mission. A hidden reason must lie behind my giving medicine to sick people. I probably hoped to seduce people to my evil Western ways. I should not be allowed to stay. But the maliks told him his words were unwise. Shahid is aware that some people do not like my living in Thull and want me to leave. He will try to counteract their influence by speaking in my behalf in the mosque.

May 29

Gul Shah came this evening to share tea and talk. He asked how Christians pray, beginning the conversation with the observation that Christianity and Islam are very close. I started with the Lord's Prayer. What a mistake! "No!" Gul Shah said. "God is not a father! He does not have children!" I tried to explain that I didn't believe God was literally my father, but that got nowhere. The entire conversation degenerated into a conversion harangue, Gul Shah trying to convert me to Islam with threats of hell and promises of paradise.

Shahid feels such discussions are dangerous and can only help our opponents. He's probably right. It did underscore the nature of argument in Thull. Reasoning starts with the Koran. One must find Koranic verses to support his position, and argue from there. The person quoting the more convincing verses usually wins the argument.

May 30

I had a good session with Anwar today. I gathered a lot of language information, and some really detailed data on herding. Unfortunately Dilaram Sher's son (I call him little Dilaram Sher) came at the end. What a giant pain in the ass that kid is! He berated Anwar for telling me the "secrets" of Thull, saying that people would kill him if they discovered what he was telling me. The situation got ugly. After Anwar left, Shahid and I continued to argue with little Dilaram Sher for some time. Finally, he admitted that he disliked Anwar because Shahid and I spent more time with Anwar than with him. He said he was only teasing Anwar about people killing him, but I'm not so sure. I was really pissed by the entire affair!

June 1

Today began hazy, hot, and humid, but then a weather front moved through, and we had a heavy rain and hail storm lasting most of the day. My mood matched the day—gloomy, morose, and cold. About all I accomplished was getting the kitchen organized and finishing War and Peace. Although it was an amazing book—probably the best I've ever read, I am sorry I read it in a way. It made me question what I'm doing here by making me think about the meaning of love and death in my own life. Do I really want to spend a significant part of my life with the people of Thull, who seem so xenophobic, narrow-minded, and violent to me?

June 8

Today we returned to Golam Sarwar's house. We all sat on a wooden platform built under a huge walnut tree. The setting was very beautiful. I hoped to get some information from Golam Sarwar's father, Akbar Shah Malik, about life in Thull during the time of the Nawab. But, although we were warmly greeted, Akbar Shah Malik refused to answer my questions. Anwar explained that many people in Thull believe I have a secret reason for asking questions. Any information I gather will be bad for the community, they say, because I am a Kafir. Some of these men told Akbar Shah Malik to tell me nothing. Shahid tried to convince him otherwise and seemed to succeed. But, this was not the time to ask more questions. Anwar said we could get the information at a later time. I learned in the course of the conversation that many people in Thull think I am a foreigner who lived in Swat Kohistan for many years. He was much disliked by the people there because he allegedly stole their trees. In the dead of night he secretly marked them, and used these marks to prove the trees belonged to his ancestors.

People believe I am this man because I told Dilaram Sher about a short visit I made to Swat Kohistan in 1980. In fact, a number of Anwar's opponents have threatened to kill him. They say he helps me gather information that will allow me to plunder the community. Anwar said that his enemies are welcome to kill him . . . if they can. He fears no one.

Later today Shahid attended the small mosque near our house. There he confronted similar rumors in the discussion that followed the afternoon prayer. Men also demanded to know why he continued to work for me if he wasn't able to convert me to Islam. He thinks he convinced them, but only twelve men were present.

June 10

Shahid and I walked to the small mosque near our house in the morning. I sat on the grass outside the mosque while he prayed with the men gathered there. My presence caused another ugly incident. Some men in the mosque complained about the Kafir (me) walking in their village and sitting outside their mosque. One old son-of-a-bitch called me a "kafrot," a word with the same connotation as "nigger" or "spic." But the *mullana* of the mosque referred to me as a "person of the book," and said to those present that it was all right for Muslims to associate with me. Wonderful! I find it interesting that he wants me to buy prayer rugs for his mosque. And he said this after I had given him worm medicine for his son. Am I being cynical?

July 5

It was a beautiful evening last night—except for the bugs biting the shit out of me! Today we drove to Kalkot to get mail. While we were there, we met the *mullana* of the main Kalkot mosque. He spent many years outside Kohistan in other parts of Pakistan and impressed both Shahid and me with his intelligence and perception. He understood what I was trying to do, having read books in Urdu about the United States.

Later we walked to Qai Afsal's house in Kallan. I was glad to get some exercise. Qai Afsal's arm has become infected from his bullet wound. I changed the bandages and gave him some antibiotics. We met Golam Sarwar's elder brother Mamad Sali (accompanied by a large group of men—about fifteen or so—all armed to the teeth) on our return. He had been visiting Anwar in Thull Proper. Later, after evening prayer, he came to our guest room to talk. What follows is the gist of the conversation.

Mamad Sali said that we should not trust most people in Thull. They may be friendly to our face, but behind our backs they are opponents.

Dilaram Sher, Gul Shah, and Anwar are good examples of such people. Anwar, he said, remains silent when others complain of my presence in Thull. He is probably not a true ally but pretends to be our friend for personal gain. Only he, Mamad Sali, and his brothers are our unqualified supporters. He and his brothers, he said, will be at our side (actually, I think he meant Shahid's side rather than mine) whenever we need assistance. He took a bullet from his cartridge belt and gave it to Shahid. "This bullet will protect you from those bad people," he said, pointing to Thull Proper. "If you are in Islamabad, Chitral, or even Russia, I will secretly come whenever you need my help."

Mamad Sali seemed sincere. He punctuated his speech with recitations from the *Kalima* and even touched Shahid's beard, a sign of respect. But what does this really mean? It's easy to believe that Dilaram Sher and even Gul Shah are not completely trustworthy. After all, they are politicians and have to butter both sides of their bread. But Anwar? He has proven invaluable as an informant, even if he receives a modest salary in return. In any case, he is a poor man with no strong political support in Thull. He cannot publicly support me. I am amazed that he has continued to work with me in the face of widespread criticism and even death threats.

July 6

Golam Sarwar, along with a number of his brothers and Anwar came to visit. Afterward, Mir Said (one of the owners of our house) complained about their presence. Golam Sarwar, he said, has joined the *dala* of Khan Akbar, Qai Afsal's *dushman*. Qai Afsal is very serious about *dushmani,* and if he were to discover that Golam Sarwar were in our house, he might come here to kill him. Because Qai Afsal's sister lives in our house (she is married to Mir Said), no one could deny him entrance. If he and Golam Sarwar were to meet in our house, the two would try to kill one another. Mir Said then gave me a detailed history of the dispute.

Shahid and I discussed the situation late into the night and were unable to decide on a good plan of action. We are caught right in the middle. Probably our best plan is to keep good relations with both sides, but how to do this is neither apparent nor easy. In any case we may lose the support of everybody as a result. Perhaps we should distance ourselves from both Qai Afsal and Golam Sarwar. But Anwar is an ally of Golam Sarwar, and he is my best informant. If both he, my informant, and Mir Said, my landlord, become actively involved on opposite sides in this blood feud, then I will be in serious trouble.

July 9

We were invited to lunch at Gul Mir's house today. He is a teacher at the school, and a relative of both Gul Shah and Qai Afsal. He is a very charming guy. I like him a lot. He sent us a formal invitation written in English. It read: "Gul Mir and his family requests the pleasure of your company for lunch at 1:00 P.M. Regrets only, but please do not disappoint me." I can't figure out where he got the words for the invitation.

We were late for lunch because Shahid stayed at the mosque after the noon prayer arguing with the people there—about thirty men. They said that Muslims should have nothing to do with Kafirs, and therefore I should leave Thull. In fact, they said, all Kafirs should leave Pakistan. Shahid believes he convinced everybody but one man that this was un-Islamic. The *mullana* of the mosque was very supportive of us.

July 11

Gul Mir and Gul Shah came to lunch today. Anwar, Mir Said, and his brother Azim Sher also ate with us. Gul Mir and Gul Shah brought their wives to eat with Abida. This is a great honor. Gul Mir and Gul Shah are known to be pious Muslims, and rarely allow their wives to visit a house which does not belong to close kinsmen.

Shahid wrote the invitation to Gul Shah and Gul Mir in Kohistani and gave it to Anwar to deliver. Our hope is that the invitation will become public knowledge and that everyone will know we have good relations with Gul Mir and Gul Shah. This will strengthen our position in Thull, since it will assure the political support of two respected men.

Later a man at the mosque told Shahid that many people have called for Anwar's death because he helps me. Anwar claimed that they cannot threaten him to his face, but he will have to take special precautions at night to make sure no one kills him.

July 12

Hazarat Fakir, Azim Sher's twelve-year-old son, has been spending a lot of time with me. He is a nice kid. He talks to me in Kohistani, which is a great help in learning the language. He also volunteers to run errands, and he even swept the floor in front of my room. But my moods continue to fluctuate wildly. Sometimes I feel positive about the research, and sometimes I feel like shit-canning the whole thing.

July 13

Gul Mir came early in the morning and talked with Shahid and me for a few hours. We showed him various books by anthropologists about the Northwest Frontier. He reads simple English; hopefully the books helped him understand what I am trying to do in Thull. Later Anwar, Mamad Sali, and some other Akbaror joined us. I spoke in my simple Kohistani and even made some mindless jokes, which seemed to please them. Shahid showed them the books, and Gul Mir argued our case as well.

Hazrat Fakir with the author

In the afternoon we went to the house of a man whose grandfather had written a history of Thull. When we arrived he made Shahid promise to tell no one the secrets of the book, especially me. If Shahid were to tell me anything, he would find him in the afterlife and kill him. I suppose everyone in the afterlife is already dead, but how to kill a dead person didn't seem to bother him. We had already gathered the stories from other people, as it turned out.

We talked to Anwar about the situation in the evening. He said that a large group of men actively oppose my living in Thull because I am a Kafir. They pressure everyone who has any contact with us. They have threatened to kill him. And after Gul Mir came for lunch, they spoke to his father, saying, "Your son has become a bad man by taking his wife to the house of a Kafir." Everyone except himself, Anwar said, will only talk to me in secret. "I have a big heart, but everyone else is afraid."

July 14

Anwar didn't come for our language lesson today. I don't know why. Shahid and I spent most of the afternoon at the school trying to explain my purpose to the teachers. Gul Mir joined the discussion on our side. He seems solidly behind us now.

Later Shahid and I discussed writing an article for one of the Pakistani newspapers, *The Daily Jang*. I would write the article in English and he would translate it to Urdu. It would describe some of the problems in Kohistan and specify how the government could help the people of Thull. Hopefully this will allay suspicions against me.

Every evening a herd of goats comes down the road. I learned that most families in the community keep a few animals during the summer which constitute this herd. I should get some pictures.

July 17

I spent a good part of the day eliciting detailed information on prayer. It's quite complex. I also learned about the *Tablighi Jamma'at,* the brotherhood of preachers. Later Golam Sarwar, Anwar, and a number of Golam Sarwar's brothers walked with Shahid and me to the mosque. I was pleasantly surprised that everyone there greeted me warmly. Perhaps our efforts are working, and I will be able to pull off this research.

July 21

While I was talking with Shahid about our situation in Thull, Mir Said came into the room, moving so silently I didn't hear him. He pointed to me and said to Shahid, "*murda.*" *Murda* means a man who is as worthless as a dead person. Mir Said seriously insulted me, for the word is only used for the most despised people.

Strangely, the incident had little effect on me. I guess I'm resigned to Thull. Even though this is a difficult place to do fieldwork, I see a fascinating research project here. And, Julé (a friend from the U.S.) is coming soon, so I won't feel so isolated.

I had an interesting talk with a man from Kalkot. He told me the reason the men of Thull are so contentious is that they don't have anything to do. Their wives do most of the farming and they fight with one another to keep from being bored. I would love to get some revenge by expounding this argument in a publication, but, unfortunately, I don't think it really works. Shit! I'm thinking about revenge! Thull is getting to me more than I realized.

July 23

Anwar came late in the afternoon. We talked about honor and what I would call "personal integrity." In the course of the conversation he said that people in Thull appear less suspicious now and that few men threaten him for working with me. But, in any case, I have become more resigned. The false rumors, lies, and hostility go with the territory here. I have to expect them.

My attempt at winning friends through newspaper writing had an interesting outcome. Rumor has it that my piece in *The Daily Jang* named the most influential *malik*s in town (which in itself is a complete fabrication). My alleged purpose in doing so was to help government officials meddle in community affairs more effectively.

July 26

We went to Abdul Rashad's house for lunch today. I met him earlier when he came to our house for medicine. He told me that some years ago an American official from the consulate in Peshawar came to the valley as his guest. After ten days, however, a *jirga* forced him to leave. Because he is a Kafir, they said, he must be in Thull for some evil reason. The people of Thull "bear me," as he put it, only because of Shahid's efforts in the mosque. Do I really need this?!

Late in the afternoon little Dilaram Sher brought two English tourists, a man and his wife, to our house. They had trekked across the pass from Swat Kohistan expecting to find a hotel, or at worst a guest house. They were lucky to find me. Thull is dangerous for anyone alone, unarmed, and outside at night.

The contrast between Swat, with its beautiful hotels and well-developed tourist trade, and Thull shocked both of them. The man was particularly disturbed by the number of weapons he saw on the Dir side of the pass. Both were typical Western tourists, with no understanding of local culture, and no idea that such an understanding might be appropriate. The man was dressed in Tyrolean knickers, and the woman wore pants—as if they were on an outing in the Swiss Alps. Neither understood that such clothing marked them as people with bad taste and no morals. To make matters worse, the woman shook hands with all the men of the house, and then lit a cigarette. Even little Hazarat Fakir was shocked. He grimaced and said to me, "That is a very bad woman!"

We talked that evening about Kohistani culture and how the people of Thull interpret Western manners, but to no avail. The conversation ended when the man said, "I'll wear knickers if I bloody well please! What right do they have to tell me what to wear?! They are just ignorant savages!"

July 28

This morning, as the English couple was about to board the bus to Dir town, the woman offered me her hand in front of all the people gathered there. Apparently our discussion about how Kohistanis interpret men and women shaking hands hadn't made much impression. I ignored it, which I know is bad manners in Euro-American terms. It must have been an interesting bus trip . . . the English looking at the Kohistanis as a bunch of ignorant religious fanatics, and the Kohistanis looking at the English as decadent spawns of the devil. Is there any hope for the world? Yet the people of Thull think I am a spawn of the devil even though I don't wear knickers and don't shake hands with women (at least in Kohistan). Perhaps I should have shaken her hand.

The "chairman" of the district council visited Thull later today. It was a big *jirga*, lots of people and lots of food. Mamad Sali greeted me warmly with an embrace in front of the gathering, a public statement of his political support, and the support of Akbaror. Later, though, a group of men referred to me, using the Kohistani words for *shit* and *piss*, thinking I didn't understand. At that moment, I wished I owned an AK-47 myself. Imagining their blood splattered on the ground in front of me was somehow comforting. Perhaps that's the way black people feel at home.

July 28–30

Shahid, Anwar, and I traveled in Swat with a Fullbright delegation of American teachers—mostly from junior colleges. I liked being with Americans, especially talking and eating with a group that included both men and women. Yet it felt strange, almost ungrammatical. I'm not sure how Anwar made sense of us. I enjoyed speaking with the Kohistanis we encountered in Swat Kohistan. They seemed surprised and genuinely pleased that I spoke their language, if only at a very rudimentary level. They appeared different from the Kohistanis in Dir—less tense and more open. Women observed *purdah* less strictly as well. Many did not cover their faces, and some even waved to the people in the bus. Anwar said the people in Swat Kohistan are members of a different religious sect than those in Thull. Perhaps this is significant. I noticed few men carrying guns, and I saw no assault rifles. A comparative study of communities in the two valleys would be interesting.

August 1

We returned to Thull yesterday, and spent most of today preparing a feast for twelve guests. The meal seemed a success, but the *mullana* from the main mosque in Thull did not come. He always appears unfriendly to me. We did send him a plate of food which he accepted and enjoyed, by all reports.

After the meal a man came to our house for medicine. He told us that many people say I went to the neighboring village of Kinorlam to take pictures of women. If this rumor gains credibility, I could be in serious trouble.

August 5

This was probably my worst day in Thull! It began when a relative of Dilaram Sher, a shopkeeper named Azim Khan, came to our house with Abdul Shashmir. Azim Khan had been in Swat Kohistan while we were there with the Fullbright delegation. During his visit, a *malik* from one of the Swat villages gave him a letter addressed to the people of Thull, with instructions to deliver it to the *mullana* of the main mosque. The letter was signed by men from three villages in Swat. The *mullana* was to read the letter to all those gathered for Friday prayer.

Azim Khan, however, showed the letter to Abdul Shashmir, who reads Urdu, to discover its contents. According to him, they are as follows: the people of Swat Kohistan lost their forests because of a foreigner who lived in their midst for a number of years. I was a friend of that foreigner and would cause the people of Thull to lose their forests as well. Therefore I should be asked to leave Thull.

Abdul Shashmir convinced Azim Khan to ignore the instructions. He reasoned that if the letter became public, Dilaram Sher's political position would be damaged. His enemies would claim that he had plotted with a Kafir to steal the forests because he, Dilaram Sher, had originally sponsored me. Azim Khan promised to bring the letter to Shahid so we can learn its exact contents.

Later that evening I tried to photograph the goat herd that passes our house each day, but the light was insufficient. What a mistake that was! About fifteen minutes later a man came to the door of our house, furiously angry because the shepherd of the herd told him I had taken pictures of his wife. I gathered that he and his wife were walking on the road a short distance behind the herd.

The situation was tense, to say the least, because the man aggressively waved his rifle at me. But, it was not without a humorous side. "I took pictures of goats, not women!" I said, and handed him my camera. "Take the film!" First, he looked into the lens, and, when I showed him the viewfinder, he looked into that, trying to find his wife inside my camera. After peering intently into the viewfinder for a few minutes, he returned the camera, said with a smile, "She is not in there," and left.

A friend offered to kill the shepherd before he spreads the lie that I photograph women. But I refused the offer. As angry and disgusted as I am at that motherfucker, I don't want to be responsible for his murder. Finally, I learned tonight about another rumor making the rounds. Some people claim I photographed especially beautiful boys at the *jirga* held for the "chairman" of the district council last week. For some reason, that one pisses me off the most.

I don't know what the result of all this will be. Right now, though, continuing to work here appears difficult. Perhaps I should begin a comparative study in Swat Kohistan.

August 8

Thull delights in torturing me. When the situation seems good, bam!, a load of shit drops on my head. And, conversely, when my position seems hopeless, something turns it around. This morning Azim Khan brought the letter allegedly from the *malik*s in Swat. It was addressed to "The people of Thull" and signed by "The people of Ushu, Utrot, and Kallam" (three villages in Swat Kohistan). No one signed the letter by name, interestingly enough. Roughly translated, the letter said:

> A foreigner came to Swat Kohistan some years previously as part of a government development project. He promised the Kohistani people his work would benefit them. But the government took Kohistani land as a result of his work, and a number of men were killed in fights with the police over the loss of this land. The foreigner living in your village does the same kind of work and will cause you to lose your land as well. Therefore, you should ask him politely to leave.

Shahid and I talked with Azim Khan at some length about what we should do. I felt we should face the issue honestly by taking the letter to the *mullana* and explaining why it was untrue. Azim Khan looked at me as though I were an incredibly stupid child. "You people are crazy!," he said. "That will only cause trouble!" And he leaped from his string bed, grabbed the letter from Shahid's hands, and tore it into small pieces. "I am only a shopkeeper, but I am no *malik*'s messenger boy! I am a *badmash* ("dangerous man") when aroused!"

We talked to Anwar about the incident after Azim Khan had left. He said that sending a letter was not customary. In cases like this, a *malik* from each of the villages in Swat Kohistan would be appointed to a delegation to visit Thull. The *malik*s of Thull would convene a *jirga* after the visitors arrived, and I would be called to answer the charges. The letter could not come from all the people in Ushu, Utrot, and Kallam because this had not happened.

Who exactly sent the letter remains a mystery. Anwar heard nothing about it from his friends in Swat while we were there. Nevertheless the incident brings into relief some interesting ethnography. Delivering the letter to the *mullana* was critical, for it would have neatly circumvented the traditional political arrangements described by Anwar. This is an effective political strategy now (whereas it probably was not in earlier years) because it plays on the growing tension between traditional, secular authority and the expanding power of religious leaders. Thus, perhaps, the incident is one more manifestation of the changing political order.

August 15

This morning the *mullana* who teaches Islamic studies at the school invited me to his house. His son was sick with a stomach ailment and he asked me for medical advice. This man always appeared unfriendly whenever I visited the school, but the other teachers assured me he is one of my biggest supporters in Thull. They say he is a man much respected for his piety, wisdom, and learning. Gul Mir said his invitation honored me.

My place in the village seems more secure these days. Abdul Rashad came for a short visit this afternoon and said that most people understand that I do not intend to hurt the community. Perhaps all our politicking worked. Tomorrow I leave for Islamabad to meet Julé.

September 2

We arrived in Thull last night. I stayed in Islamabad longer than expected because the engine in my jeep needed repairs. Julé brought some toys for the kids in our house, which seemed to make a big hit. But the flea bombs she brought were a complete failure. Even with the bombs and insect repellant the bugs still bit the shit out of us!

September 7

Today Shahid and I went to Gul Makhmud's house (a man from Kallan) to discuss funding for a mosque. The Dutch Government has a grant program that dispenses small amounts of money to local communities, and I had offered to help with the application. About fifteen men were present, elders as well as younger men.

When we finished discussing the application, I asked the elders about life in Thull during the reign of the last Nawab. They all refused to answer at first, as if I had asked them to tell me where they had hid their life savings. Finally, Gul Makhmud convinced his father my question was harmless, and he reluctantly responded. Later Abdul Shashmir explained their reaction. They suspect my secret mission is gathering information to help the government register land. Consequently they believe anything I learn about Thull will cause men to lose their property and the community to lose its political independence. Most people were glad, therefore, when I stayed in

Islamabad, but are unhappy now that I have returned to Thull. Hajji Jan Azgul even accused Anwar of "pulling down the shawl of the village" by teaching me Kohistani. I always thought he and I were on good terms. What more can I do? All these months, and people despise and suspect me now as much as they did when I first arrived.

Tonight Gul Shah told me the latest rumor, which made me want to laugh as much as cry. Because Julé observes *purdah* and Western women do not, she must be Muslim. Hence, I married a Muslim, which is a serious wrongdoing since Islam expressly forbids Muslim women to marry Kafirs. Everything I do is turned against me. I should have shaken hands with that English woman. In fact, I should have embraced her right there in front of everybody. That would have given the assholes something to think about!

September 8

Today my work in Thull came to an inglorious end. I must say it finished in a spectacular display of fireworks. About 1:30 I opened the door of our house to a *jirga* of approximately twenty men. Shahid and I met them under the apricot tree that stands like a sentinel at the entrance to our house. Anger twisted their faces, which told me immediately I was up a rat's ass.

"And here comes the shit!," I thought.

One man spoke for the group. Refusing to meet my eyes, he instead hurled his words at my feet.

"God," he said, "no longer gives his blessing to Thull because of the *kafrot*. The foreigner must leave!"

At first, Shahid tried to change their minds, but that was a task more Herculean than cleaning horse manure from the Augean stables. Finally, he declared, "Our living in the village is for the *malik*s to decide! They should come to our house and tell us if we can stay!"

Then, turning our backs (I imagined flipping them the bird, but of course they wouldn't have understood that), we stalked into our house—rather quickly, I might add. I slammed the door in their surprised faces in a gesture of meaningless defiance.

The *malik*s never came. Instead a much larger and more angry crowd returned about a half hour later. This time Azim Sher, the eldest of our three landlords, ordered Shahid and me to remain inside, and he faced the crowd alone. Well . . . not quite alone. A few of his kin joined the crowd to give him support if he needed it. And, it soon became obvious he needed it. The scene grew increasingly ugly. Demands that I leave became more insistent, and insults hurled at Azim Sher more vituperation. Finally, one man spurred the crowd to shatter the door of the house and attack Julé. But Azim Sher's brother-in-law stepped in front of the door saying, "This is the house of my sister. Anyone who enters will eat my bullets!" I knew then that my work in Thull was over because if I stayed someone would die—quite possibly me! Shahid and I left the house to face our opponents.

"Maa bacha?!" which translates, "we will leave!" I said. And with as much dignity as we could muster, Shahid and I strategically withdrew behind the walls of our house. (Actually we beat a rather hasty, if not cowardly, retreat—much like two microbes trying to escape a shot of penicillin!) Immediately, the crowd dispersed, my opponents to savor their victory as they returned to their lairs in the village.

My journal stops here, but my stay in Thull did not end for another week. Several days earlier my jeep driver took the bus to Rawalpindi to visit his family. He never returned to Thull. Later I learned he was in jail, arrested for auto theft. This gave me time to gather some much-needed information from the few allies who remained loyal.

Anwar came to my house to show his loyalty fifteen minutes after the crowd left; Gul Shah invited Shahid and me to lunch, a public statement of his support; and Mamad Sali appeared at our door a few days later.

"I would have come earlier," he explained, "but my father is sick and will die soon. Come to my house to live. No one can say anything to me. I have too many rifles behind me."

The offer was tempting, but I declined, for that would have surely involved the Akbaror in a war, and people would have died. I could not have someone's death on my conscience, even if it were the death of an opponent.

Dilaram Sher invited me to supper, but ever the politician, he spirited me to his house a few hours after dark so no one would see. And the *malik*s finally came—in a group of ten. But they came only to ask that I not use my influence with the District Commissioner to punish Thull. They believed to the very end I was a government agent and therefore possessed a special relationship with the District Commissioner.

I began to understand these events more clearly in the days that followed. My opponents accused me of taking pictures of women, using the shepherd's charges as proof. Photographing women is a serious transgression against Islamic morality, and consequently many believed I had turned God against them. On the surface, at least, this was why they demanded I leave. At times my darker self regretted not accepting my friend's offer to kill the shepherd, I must admit. At the same time, this incident—in which I was an active, if unwilling, participant—clarified some of the more murky features of Kohistani politics.

Because photographing women is a sin, my living in Thull became enmeshed in the greater *jihad.* Consequently it was a religious, rather than secular, issue and therefore inappropriate for secular authorities to decide. Hence Shahid's demand that *malik*s decide my fate was inappropriate, and thus ignored. Furthermore the charge against me, whose legitimacy the government could not deny, gave my opponents a reason to demand that I leave Thull. My opponents thereby rid themselves of someone they believed was a dangerous government spy by appealing to a morality the government itself professed. I had to admire the cleverness of the ploy.

Beyond illustrating clever ploys, however, the events express interwoven tensions inherent in Kohistani politics today—tensions between government bureaucrats and village leaders, between *maliks* and *mullanas*, and between those whose power is rooted within village communities and those whose power draws on the outside world. Dilaram Sher and Gul Shah, my most politically powerful supporters, depend on timber contracts with the Pakistani government. If I were a government agent, my good will could be turned to their benefit. Hajji Jan Azgul and Hajji Daud Khan, two of my most powerful opponents, base their economic power on farming and herding. Hence land registration threatened their power by threatening their land holdings. If I had been a government agent, I posed a serious danger to them. Not surprisingly, therefore, they encouraged the shepherd to spread his accusations.

When the story of my photographing women became widespread in Thull, the *mullanas'* hands were forced. If they declined to speak against me, then they risked weakening their claim to political authority in the greater *jihad*. Thus, *maliks* forced *mullanas* to use religious authority for the *maliks'* secular aims. But this was only an effective strategy because of the changing nature of Kohistani politics. My experiences helped me see how rivalries between opposing *maliks*, oppositions between *maliks* and the government, and tensions between secular and religious authorities twisted around one another. In the process I began to understand the changing nature of politics in Thull.

Thursday came and still no sign of our driver. Friends reported that my opponents planned to launch an armed attack after noon prayer on Friday. Our three landlords spent Thursday evening carefully cleaning and loading

A landlord checks his rifle preparing to defend our house

their rifles and filling cartridge belts with bullets to prepare for the upcoming battle. The women in the house showed Julé and Abida a hidden path to a hiding place in an adjacent cornfield where they could safely hide from stray bullets. For the first time I feared for our safety.

Early on Friday morning, however, Shahid walked to Thull Proper and found a visiting truck driver, who agreed to drive us to Dir town. But of course, for the first time since I owned it, the jeep refused to start. After a few pushes down nearby hills the engine finally caught, and we left Thull about an hour before the impending attack.

I returned a week later to collect our possessions. Mir Said asked that we stay, saying he would call a *jirga* of the entire community to decide the issue. But I had arranged to begin research in another Kohistani community, and declined his offer.

I often thought about Thull during my stay in Shanku, a Kohistani village in the Swat Valley. Shanku was different from Thull. Few people were armed, and then only with shotguns and pistols; music was an important part of village life, especially in communal work groups; and *purdah* was less stringently observed. Most importantly, people in Shanku related to me differently. They seemed more friendly and accepting. Julé and I often walked in the mountains surrounding Shanku, and many people we met asked us to share food in their houses. One man even touched my beard during a visit to his house, a sign of respect I was never accorded in Thull. I concluded that people in Shanku were more humane, probably because of differences in religious sect.

I don't believe this any longer. No motorable road leads to Shanku as it does to Thull. Consequently timbering was a minor economic activity. As a possible tree thief, therefore, I posed little threat to people's livelihood. More importantly, the Swat Government already registered land, so no one could suspect me of gathering information for that purpose. People in Shanku could treat me with more openness and friendliness because I did not threaten them.

In contrast, I troubled Thull because of the economic and political situation in Dir. The government there *is* trying to reduce timber royalties and *is* trying to force land registration. Families face severe economic losses if administrators succeed in instituting these policies. The people of Thull knew the government sponsored my work. Hence their suspicions were realistic, though mistaken. People in Shanku would probably act similarly in analogous situations.

And the men of Thull granted me humanity. They suspected I was a government spy, and treated me accordingly. Yet this proclaimed my status as a man, not much different from them. For underneath their suspicions lay the assumption that secret motives and selfish purposes equally inspire everyone. They did not say, as we often say, "He is alien, therefore, inscrutable." No. They understood, if in a twisted way, that sometimes behind the surface elaborations of culture lies obscured our common humanness.

Bibliography

Averill, James R.
  1982 *Anger and Aggression: An Essay on Emotion.* New York: Springer-Verlag.
Barth, Fredrik
  1956 *Indus and Swat Kohistan.* Oslo: Forenede Trykkerier.
  1959 *Political Leadership Among Swat Pathans.* London: Athlone.
Beattie, John
  1964 *Other Cultures.* London: Routledge and Kegan Paul.
Biddulph, John
  1971 (1880) *Tribes of the Hindoo Koosh.* Graz: Akademische Druck- u. Verlagsanstalt.
Black-Michaud, Jacob
  1975 *Cohesive Force.* New York: St. Martin's Press.
Boehm, Christopher
  1984 *Blood Revenge.* Lawrence: University of Kansas Press.
Chagnon, Napolean A.
  1988 "Life Histories, Blood Revenge, and Warfare in a Tribal Population." *Science* 239:935–992.
  1989 "Response to Ferguson." *American Ethnologist* 16, no. 3:565–569.
Davies, C. Collin
  1932 *The Problem of the North-West Frontier 1890–1908: With a Survey of Policy Since 1849.* Cambridge: Cambridge University Press.
Djilas, Milovan
  1958 *Land Without Justice.* New York: Harcourt Brace.
Evans-Pritchard, E. E.
  1940 *The Nuer.* Oxford: Oxford University Press.
Ferguson, R. Brian, and Leslie E. Farragher
  1988 *The Anthropology of War: A Bibliography,* Number One. Occasional Papers of the Harry Frank Guggenheim Foundation. New York: Harry Guggenheim Foundation.

Hallpike, Christopher
1977   *Bloodshed and Vengeance in the Papuan Mountains.* Oxford: Clarendon Press.

Harré, Rom (ed.)
1986   *The Social Construction of Emotions.* Oxford: Basil Blackwell.

Howard, Robert E.
1934   "The People of the Black Circle." *Weird Tales* (September, October, November). [Also published in *The Sword of Conan,* by Robert E. Howard, New York: The Gnome Press (1952), and *Conan the Adventurer,* by Robert E. Howard and L. Sprague De Camp, New York: Ace Books (1966)].

Keiser, R. Lincoln
1986   "Rim Shots and Rifle Fire." *Natural History* 95, no. 9:26–32.

Lawrence, Elizabeth A.
1982   *Rodeo.* Chicago: The University of Chicago Press.

Leach, E. R.
1954   (1964 edition). *Political Systems of Highland Burma.* Boston: Beacon Press.

Lutz, Catherine A.
1988   *Unnatural Emotions.* Chicago: The University of Chicago Press.

McMahon, A. H., and A. D. G. Ramsay
1981 (1901)   *Report on the Tribes of Dir, Swat and Bajour.* Peshawar: Saeed Book Bank. [Originally published in India by The Government Printing Office.]

Meeker, Michael
1980   "The Twilight of a South Asian Heroic Age." *Man* (n.s.) 14, no. 4:682–701.

Metcalf, Barbara Daly
1984   "Islamic Reform and Islamic Women: Maulana Thanawi's *Jewelry of Paradise.*" In *Moral Conduct and Authority* edited by Barbara Daly Metcalf. Berkeley: The University of California Press.

Pennell, Dr. T. L.
1913   *Among the Wild Tribes of the Afghan Frontier.* London: Seeley, Service and Co.

Pitt-Rivers, Julian
1977   *The Fate of Shachem or the Politics of Sex.* Cambridge: Cambridge University Press.

Robertson, Sir George Scott
1896   *The Kafirs of the Hindu-Kush.* London: Lawrence and Bullen.

Rosaldo, Renato
1984   "Grief and the Headhunter's Rage." In *Text, Play, and Story,* edited by Edward M. Bruner. Prospect Heights, IL: Waveland Press.

Sagen, Carl
1977   *The Dragons of Eden.* New York: Random House.

Shahrani, Nasif, and Robert Canfield
1984   *Revolutions and Rebellions in Afghanistan.* Berkeley: Institute of International Studies.

Glossary

aizzat: honor in the sense of prestige
aman pasand: peace lover, a man who works for peaceful relationships within a
    community
asar: afternoon prayer (*namaz*)
azan: the call to *namaz* prayer
babatani: close agnates (lit., father-selves)
badal: revenge
baghrairat: without honor or self integrity
baghrairatman: person without self integrity
banal: a summer pasture with a distinct boundary and name
chare: digging implement similar to a spade, but operated by two people
dadatani: distant agnates (lit., grandfather-selves)
dala: political bloc, faction, or party
dalabasi: opposition between parties
dosotani: friends (lit., friend-selves)
du'a: prayer said at special occasions, for example, after meals or upon initiating a
    building project
dum: patrilineal descent group
dushman: enemy
dushmani: enmity
fajar: morning prayer (*namaz*)
gan, gin: (m., f.) big
ghrairat: honor in the sense of self integrity
imam: leader of a mosque
iman: Muslim faith
isha: night prayer (*namaz*)
isotani: wife's agnates (lit. wife-selves)
ja: brother
jar: dispute
jihad: struggle against evil
jirga: usually a town council, but, any political meeting
kafir: pagan, infidel
kafrot: pagan, infidel, but used as an insult
kalima: Muslim affirmation of faith
kohistan: land of mountains

125

kohistani: native term for the language spoken in Swat and Dir Kohistan. It is sometimes called Garvi in Swat Kohistan
kohistanis: inhabitants of Kohistan
lamo aman: village or community peace
likit, lukut: (m., f.) small
lud: group sharing pasture rights
lukut, likit: (m., f.) small
madrasa: religious school
maghrib: evening prayer (*namaz*)
malik: a man of influence, secular leader
mar dushmani: death enmity
maxilaf: opponent
momotani: mother's agnates (lit. mother-selves)
mullah: low ranking religious authority
mullana: high ranking religious authority
mulvi: middle ranking religious authority
mushrik: person who believes in saints
musselman: Muslim
namaz: prayer said five times each day
nawab: king or chief
pakhtun: ethnic group dominating the Northwest Frontier Province of Pakistan
pakhtunwali: code of the Pakhtuns
pathan: popular name for Pakhtun originating in India
pushto: language of the Pakhtuns
purdah: seclusion of women
qaom: political community
rakat: ritual unit of *namaz* prayer
ramazan: month of fasting called *Ramadan* in the western part of the Muslim world
rashagat: anger
sharam: shame in the sense of sexual modesty
tablighi: member of the tablighi Jamma't
tablighi Jamma't: a political organization espousing fundamentalist Islam (lit. community of preachers or evangelists)
zohar: noon prayer (*namaz*)

Index